Joseph Ritson, William Carew Hazlitt

Ancient Songs and Ballads from King Henry the Second to the Revolution

Joseph Ritson, William Carew Hazlitt

Ancient Songs and Ballads from King Henry the Second to the Revolution

ISBN/EAN: 9783743397606

Manufactured in Europe, USA, Canada, Australia, Japa

Cover: Foto ©ninafisch / pixelio.de

Manufactured and distributed by brebook publishing software (www.brebook.com)

Joseph Ritson, William Carew Hazlitt

Ancient Songs and Ballads from King Henry the Second to the Revolution

Ancient Songs

AND

Ballads,

FROM

THE REIGN OF KING HENRY THE SECOND
TO THE REVOLUTION.

COLLECTED BY

JOSEPH RITSON, ESQ.

IN TWO VOLUMES.

VOL. II.

I love a ballad but even too well.
SHAKSPEARE.

LONDON:

PRINTED FOR PAYNE AND FOSS, PALL-MALL;
BY THOMAS DAVISON, WHITEFRIARS.
1829.

CONTENTS

OF

VOLUME THE SECOND.

CLASS THE THIRD.

	Page
1. Balet, by Anthony Woodvyle earl Rivers	3
2. Gramercy myn own purse	5
3. The praise of serving-men, or Troly loly	7
4. Upon the inconstancy of his mistress	10
5. Invocation to Death	12
6. A carol on bringing up a boars head to the table on Christmas-day	14
7. In die nativitatis. [a Christmas carol.]	16
8. In die nativitatis. [Another Christmas carol.]	17
9. Dialogue between two lovers	18
10. The kind lady reproaches her defamatory deserter	19
11. In praise of the joyful life of a bachelor	20
12. My swete swetyng	21
13. Mutual affection	22
14. The proffered services of affection	23

CLASS THE FOURTH.

1. The dying maidens complaint	27
2. Tye the mare, Tom boy	31
3. In dispraise of women	35
4. The discontented husband	36
5. Captain Car	38

CONTENTS.

		Page
6.	A mery ballet of the hathorne tre	44
7.	The lamentation of George Mannington	47
8.	The praise of a country-mans life	51
9.	The three ravens. A dirge	53
10.	The too courteous knight	54
11.	John Dory	57
12.	The spring-time. By Shakspeare	60
13.	The power of music. By the same	61
14.	Hark! hark! the lark. By the same	62
15.	The mothers lullaby	63
16.	The garland	64
17.	The jovial tinker	ibid.
18.	Robin, lend to me thy bow	69
19.	Floddon-Field	70
20.	The ungrateful Knight and fair Flower of Northumberland	75
21.	The heir of Linne	81
22.	Lord Thomas and fair Eleanor	89
23.	Fair Margaret and sweet William	92
24.	Batemans tragedy	95
25.	The wandering Prince of Troy	101
26.	The Spanish Ladys Love	106
27.	The Ladys Fall	110
28.	Little Musgrave and Lady Barnard	116
29.	Fair Rosamond	120
30.	The lamentation of Jane Shore	128
31.	True love requited: or, The Bailiffs daughter of Islington	134
32.	The king of France's daughter	136
33.	The famous Flower of Serving-men: or, The Lady turned Serving-man	145
34.	The Children in the Wood: or, The Norfolk gentlemans last will and testament	150
35.	George Barnwel	156
36.	King Henry the second and the Miller of Mansfield	173

CONTENTS.

	Page
37. King John and the Abbot of Canterbury	183
38. Sir Lancelot du Lake	188
39. Sir Guy of Warwick	193
40. The Honour of a London Prentice	199
41. Sir Andrew Barton	204
42. John Armstrongs Last Good Night	214
43. The Hunting in Chevy-Chase	218

CLASS THE FIFTH.

1. A love-song. By Master Wither	233
2. A carol for presenting the wassel-bowl	238
3. A Christmas carol	241
4. The taming of a shrew	242
5. Tom of Bedlam	247
6. Another Tom of Bedlam	251
7. Newes	255
8. When the king enjoys his own again	257
9. John and Joan: or, A mad couple well met	263
10. Phillida flouts me	268
11. A worshipper of cruelty	272
12. O Anthony now, now, now	273
13. The new courtier	276
14. The defeat of the Spanish Armada	280
15. The prodigals resolution; or, My father was born before me	282
16. The honest fellow	286
17. The Belgick boar	286
Glossary	295

Ancient Songs and Ballads.

CLASS III.

COMPRISING

THE REIGNS OF EDWARD IV. AND HENRY VIII.

VOL. II. B

I.

BALET, BY ANTHONY WOODVYLE EARL RIVERS.

WRITTEN DURING HIS IMPRISONMENT IN PONTEFRACT CASTLE, ANNO 1483.

This little piece is preserved by Rouse the historian, and has been reprinted by dr. Percy; but as the use of the Fairfax MS. enabled the present editor to supply a considerable chasm in the printed copies, the curious reader will not be sorry to see it complete *.

The measure, which is now properly regulated, was ordinarily adopted by song-writers, from Chaucer to Skelton.

The music of the MS. is (as usual) a composition in three parts, by dr. Fayrfax.

> Sum what musyng,
> And more mornyng,
> In remembring
> The unstydfastnes,

* [Mr. Ritson, " professing to follow" *the printed copies*, and only to supply *a chasm, in them*, from *the Fairfax MS.*:—the extract for that purpose being made with his usual accuracy, and distinguished by brackets—appears to be very unjustly charged with " discrepancies" in the publication of this ballad; which, it may be added, has been inserted *verbatim* as completed, in the fourth edition of the " *Reliques.*" Ed.]

This world being
Of such whelyng,
Me contrarieng,
    What may I gesse?

I fere dowtles,
Remediles,
Is now to sese
    My wofull chaunce
[For unkyndness,
Withouten less,
And no redress,
    Me doth avaunce.

With displesaunce,
To my grevaunce,
And no suraunce,
    Of remedy].
Lo in this traunce,
Now in substance,
Such is my dawnce,
    Willyng to dye.

Me thynkys truly
Bowndyn am I,
And that gretly,
    To be content;
Seyng playnly
That fortune doth wry
All contrary
    From myn entent.

V. 30. That *omitted. MS.*

My lyff was lent
Me to on intent,
Hytt is ny spent;
 Welcome fortune:
But I ne went,
Thus to be shent,
But sho hit ment,
 Such is hur won.   40

V. 34. To an entent. *MS.*

II.

GRAMERCY MYN OWN PURSE.

Given from the " Boke " of " hawkynge and huntynge," &c. " Enprynted at Westmestre by Wynkyn the Worde the yere of thyncarnacion of oure lorde. M.CCCC. lxxxxvi."

" Dame Julyans Bernes," the compiler of this volume, or at least the authoress of the " boke of [hawkynge and] huntynge "—for, besides this, it contains " liber armorum," " the treatyse of fysshynge wyth an angle," and " the blasynge of armes,"—is generally supposed to have been the daughter of sir James Berners of Berners-Roding in Essex, and sister to Richard lord Berners; she was prioress of the nunnery of Sopewell near St. Albans, and is said to have flourished in and about the year 1460. (See Bale, Ballards *Memoirs of British Ladies,* &c.)

After the " Explicit " of this last " boke " are some miscellaneous observations, as, " Bestys of the chace;" " The names of dyvers manere houndes;" "The propritees of a good Grehounde;" " The proprytees of a good horse;" several old curious proverbial sentences; " The companyes of bestys & foules;" " The dewe termys to speke of brekynge or dressynge of dyvers beestys & foules. &c...... And....of certen fysshes;" " The shyres and bysshopryckes [and provynces]......of Englonde." And then, but without any title or head, comes the following ballad. [sig. e. vi. b.]

The abovementioned compilation is usually termed the "Boke of St. Albans," where it was originally printed by the anonymous schoolmaster (" John Insomuch") in 1486; but the ballad here printed is not to be found in that edition.

A FAYTHFULL frende wolde I fayne fynde,
   To fynde hym there he myght be founde,
But now is the worlde wexte soo unkynde,
   That frenship is fall to the grounde:
   Now a frende I have founde
That I woll nother banne ne curse;
   But, of all frendes in felde or towne,
Ever, Gramercy, myn owne purse!

My purse it is my prevy wyf,
   This songe I dare bothe synge and saye,   10
It partyth men of moche stryfe,
   Whan every man for himself shall pay.
   As I ryde in riche aray,
For golde and sylver men woll me flouryssh,
   By this matere I dare well say,
Ever, Gramercy, myn own purse!

As I ryde wyth golde so rede,
   And have to doo wyth londys lawe,
Men for my money woll make me speede,
   And for my goodes they woll me knawe;   20
   More and lesse to me woll drawe,
Bothe the better and the wurse,
   By this matere I saye in sawe
Ever, Gramercy, myn owne purse!

It fell by me upon a tyme,
　　As it hath doo by many mo,
My horse, my nete, my shepe, my swyne,
　　And all my goodes, they fell me fro;
　　I went to my frendes and tolde theym so,
And home agayne they badde me trusse: 　30
　　I sayd agayne, whan I was wo,
Ever, Gramercy, myn owne pursse.

Therfore, I rede you, syres all,
　　To assaye your frendes or ye have nede,
For and ye come downe and have a fall,
　　Full fewe of theym for you woll grede:
Therfore, assaye theym everychone,
　　Bothe the better and the wurse.
Our lorde, that shope bothe sonne and mone,
　　Sende us spendynge in our [own] purse! 　40

III.

THE PRAISE OF SERVING-MEN,

OR

TROLY LOLY.

This song, which is given from MSS. Sloan. No. 1584, a small book, partly paper, partly parchment, chiefly written by John Gysborn, canon of Coverham, in Yorkshire, whose manual or pocket-book it seems to have been (tempore H. 8.), if it be that mentioned by Langham under the above title, has been once popular, which is the principal inducement to its insertion. In another part of the MS. we find the spark here represented, who, very probably, is the serving-man described in the song. The chorus or burden is of vast antiquity, being a great favourite with the pot-companions of Edward the thirds time, as we learn from the *Vision of Pierce Plowman:*

" And than satten some and songe at the nale,
" And holpen erie his halfe acre wyth HEY TROLLY LOLLY."

Thus too, in " the lytell propre jeste, called Cryste crosse me spede. a. b. c." printed by Wynken de Worde:

" To the ale they went with HEY TROLY LOLY."
(See Herberts Ames, 1019.)

In the *Chester Whitsun plays* (a MS. in the Museum) it is said, *Tunc cantabunt* [*pastores*], and in the margin are these words, " *Singe troly loly lo.*" But there may have been many songs with this burthen.

So well ys me begone, *Troly, lolé.*

Off serving-men I wyll begyne,
Troly, loley.

For they goo mynyon trym.
Troly, loley.

Off mett and drynk and feyr clothyng,
Troly, loley.

By dere god, I want ' nothyng.'
Troly, loley.

His bonet is of fyne scarlett,
Troly, loley.

Wyth here as black ' as gett.'
Troly, lolye.

[*V.* 8. none]   [*V.* 12. os.]

His dublett ys of fyne satyne,
    Troly, lolye.
Hys shertt well mayd and tryme.
    Troly, lolye.

Hys coytt itt is so tryme and rownde,
    Troly, lolye.
His kysse is worth a hundred pownde.   20
    Troly, lolye.

His hoysse of London-black,
    Troly, lolye.
In hyme ther ys no lack.
    Troly, lolye.

His face yt ys so lyk a man,
    Troly, lolye.
Who cane butt love hyme than?
    Troly, lolye.

Whersoever he bee, he hath my hert,   30
    Troly, lolye.
And shall 'till' deth 'do part.'
    Troly, lolye.

[*V.* 32. To deth depart.]

IV.

UPON THE INCONSTANCY OF HIS MISTRESS.

From a MS. of the early part of Henry the 8ths time. Bibl. Harl. No. 2252. Left unfinished by the copyist.

MORNYNG, mornyng,
Thus may I synge,
  Adew, my dere, adew;
Be god alone,
My love ys gon,
  Now may I go seke a new.

Nay, nay, no, no,
I wys not soo,
  Leve of and do no more;
For veraylye   10
Som wemen ther be,
  The whyche bethe brotyll store.

I lovyd on,
Not long agon,
  On whom my harte was sett,
So dyd she me,
Whye shuld I lye?
  I can hyt not forgette.

Hyr letters wyll prove
She was my love,   20
  And so I wyll hyr clayme,

Thowghe my swete-harte
Be fro me starte,
   She ys the more to blame.

Thowe my swete-harte
Be fro me starte
   And changyd me for a new,
I am content,
And wyll assente
   With hym that hath hyr now.   30

For be saynte Gyle,
And Mary mylde,
   He ys a mynion man,
Myche propyr and good,
Commyn of jentyll blode,
   And myche good pastyme he can.

He ys worthy
Myche better then I
   To have the love of hyr,
Therfor, swete-harte,   40
Farwell my parte
   Adew, somtyme my dere.

V.

INVOCATION TO DEATH.

BY GEORGE VISCOUNT ROCHFORD.

The following poem, sir John Hawkins tells us, appears by the MS. from which it was taken, to have been composed about the time of Henry VIII. It and another, which he has printed, were communicated to him by "a very judicous antiquary lately deceased," whose opinion of them was, that they were written either by, or in the person of Anne Boleyn: a conjecture, he adds, which her unfortunate history renders very probable. It is, however, but a conjecture; any other state-prisoner of that period having an equal claim. George viscount Rochford, brother to the above lady, and who suffered on her account, "hath the fame," according to Phillips, "of being the author of songs and sonnets," and to him the present editor is willing to refer the ensuing stanzas.

O Death rocke me on slepe,
  Bringe me on quiet reste,
Let passe my verye giltless goste,
  Out of my carefull brest:
Toll on the passinge-bell,
Ringe out the dolefull knell,
Let the sounde my dethe tell,
    For I must dye,
    There is no remedy,
    For now I dye.

My paynes who can expres?
   Alas! they are so stronge,
My dolor will not suffer strength
   My lyfe for to prolonge:
Toll, &c.

Alone in prison stronge,
   I wayle my destenye;
Wo worth this cruel hap that I
   Should taste this miserye!
Toll, &c.   20

Farewell my pleasures past,
   Welcum my present payne,
I fele my torments so increse[d]
   That lyefe cannot remayne:

Cease now the passing-bell,
Rong is my doleful knell,
For the sound my deth doth tell,
    Deth doth draw nye,
    Sound my end dolefully,
    For now I dye.

VI.

A CAROL ON BRINGING UP A BOARS HEAD TO THE TABLE ON CHRISTMAS-DAY.

———Printed from that eminent and excellent antiquary Thomas Hearnes "*Notæ et Spicilegium*" to William of Newborough (III. 745.), where it is thus introduced:—"I will beg leave here to give an exact copy of the Christmas Carol upon the Boar's Head (which is an ancient dish, and was brought up by K. Henry 'II.' with trumpets before his son when his said son was crowned [Hollynshed's Chron. Vol. III. p. 76.]) as I have it, in an old fragment (for I usually preserve even fragments of old books) of the Christmas Carols printed by Wynkyn de Worde,....by which it will be perceived how much the same Carol is altered as it is sung in some places even now from what it was at first*. It is the last thing, it seems, of the book (which I never yet saw intire) and at the same time I think it proper also to add the printer's conclusion, for this reason, at least, that such as write about our first printers may have some notice of the date of this book, and the exact place where printed, provided they cannot be able to meet with it, as I believe they will find it pretty difficult to do, it being much laid aside about the time that some of David's psalms came to be used in it's stead." (See also his preface to "Robert of Gloucester's chronicle," p. xiii.)

The Colophon runs thus: ¶ Thus endeth the Christmasse carolles, newely enprinted at London, in the fletestrete at the sygne of the sonne by Wynkyn de Worde. The yere of our lorde. M.D.xxi.

This antique ceremony is still observed in Queens-college, Oxford, with this considerable improvement, indeed, that the Boars head is neatly carved in wood.

The book of Psalms above referred to is in a note thus described:

---

* "An insinuation, cunningly, but plainly, levelled at the gentlemen of *Queen's*." (Wartons "*Companion to the guide*," p. 29, 30.)

"Certaine of David's Psalmes intended for Christmas Carolls fitted to the most common but solempne tunes, every where familiarly used: By William Slatyer. Printed by Robert Young 1630. 8º."
Queen Margaret, wife to James IV. of Scotland, "at the furst course" of her wedding-dinner, "was served of a wyld borres hed gylt, within a fayr platter." (Lelands *Collectanea*, 1770, iii. 294.)
The ancient crest of the family of Edgcumbe was the Boars head, crowned with bays, upon a charger; which has been very injudiciously changed into the entire animal. The partiality shown by one of this species to the late lord is the subject of a very humorous ode by the facetious Peter Pindar.

Caput apri ' defero '
Reddens ' laudes ' domino.

THE bores heed in hand bring I,
With 'garlands' gay and rosemary,
I pray you all synge merely,
   Qui estis in convivio.

The bores-head, I understande,
Is the 'chefe' servyce in this lande;
Loke where ever it be fande,
   Servite cum cantico.

Be gladde, lordes, bothe more and lasse,
  For this hath ordeyned our stewàrde,
To chere you all this christmasse,
  The bores-heed with mustàrde.

V. 1. differo.   *V.* 2. laudens.   *V.* 8. thefe.

VII.

IN DIE NATIVITATIS.

This, and the following ancient Christmas Carols, are given, merely as curiosities, from the editors folio MS., where each is accompanied with a musical composition for three voices; but which, neither in point of merit nor antiquity, seems to deserve a place in this work.

Nowel, Nowel (the old French name for Christmas), and a great cry at that period, was the usual burden to this sort of things. Many instances of which may be found in No. 2593. Bib. Sloan.

It was likewise the name of this sort of composition, which is equally ancient and popular. Books of carols were cried about the streets of Paris in the thirteenth century. "Noel, noel, *à moult grant cris.*"

> Nowell, nowell, nowell, nowell,
> Tydynges gode y thyngke to telle.
>
> The borys hede that we bryng here
> Be tokeneth a prince withowte pere,
> Ys borne this day to bye us dere,
>   Nowell.
>
> A bore ys a soverayn beste,
> And acceptab[l]e in every feste,
> So mote thys lord be to moste and leste,
>   Nowell.
>
> This borys hede we bryng with song,
> In worchyp of hym that thus sprang,
> Of a virgyne to redresse all wrong,
>   Nowell.

VIII.

IN DIE NATIVITATIS.

Nowell, Nowell, Nowell, Nowell,
Who ys ther that syngyt so, Nowell, Nowell?

I am here, syre Chrystesmasse.
Wellcome my lord syre Chrystesmasse,
Welcome to us bothe mor and lasse,
    Com ner, Nowell.

Deu vous garde, bewe syre. Tydynges y you bryng,
A mayde hath born a chylde full yong,
The weche causeth yew to syng,
    Nowell.

Criste is now born of a pure mayde,
In an oxe stalle he ys layde,
Wherefor syng we alle atte a brayde,
    Nowell.

Bevux bien, par tutte la company,
Make gode chere and be ryght mery,
And syng with us now joyfully,
    Nowell.

IX.

DIALOGUE BETWEEN TWO LOVERS.

" In which," sir J. Hawkins, from whom it is given, gravely remarks, " there is great simplicity of style and sentiment, and a frankness discoverable on the lady's part not warranted by the manners of the present time."

It likewise occurs in the old part song book, 1530, whence it has been corrected since the last edition. The music, in three parts, was by dr. Fayrfax.

" MIN hartys lust and all my plesure,
  Ys gevyn wher I maye not take yt ageyn."
" Do ye repent?" " Naye, I make you sure.".
  " What ys the cause then [that] ye do complayn?"

" It plesyth my hart to shew part of my payn."
  " To whom?" " To you." " Please that wyl not
    me;
Be all thes wordys to me, they be in vayn,
  Complayn you, wher ye may have remedy."

" I do complayn, and [can] find no relese."
  " Yee, do ye so? I pray you tel me how."
" My lady lyst not my paynys to redres."
  " Say ye soth?" " Yee, I make god a vowe."

" Who ys your lady?" " I put case you."
  " Who, I? nay, be sure, yt ys not soo."
" In fayth, ye be." " Why do ye swere now?"
  " For, in good fayth, I love you and no moo."

" No mo but me ? " " No, so sayd I."
" May I you trust ? " " Yee, I make you sure."
" I fere nay." " Yes, I shall tel you why."
" Tell on, ' let's ' here." " Ye have my hart in cure."

" Your hart ? nay." " Yes, wythout mesùre,
I do you love." " I pray yow, say not so."
" In feyth, I do." " May I of you be sure ? "
" Yee, in good fayth." " Then am I yours, allsoo."

X.

THE KIND LADY REPROACHES HER DEFAMATORY DESERTER.

  And wyll ye serve me so ?
  For my kyndnes, thus to serve me soo !

In fayth ye be to blame,
For my good wyll me to dyffame,
And therof to make a game :
  And yet to serve me so.
And wyll ye serve me so ?
For my kyndnes, thus to serve me so !

Be Crist, spare not, hardely,
I trust ons, or that I dye,
To do as moche for you, perdy ;
  And yf ye serve me soo.

And wyl ye serve me so?
For my kyndnes, thus to serve me so!

Why, then, adew, I wyll be playn:
Be sure, your company I shal refrayn,
Which, at length, shall be to your payn:
　I fors not though ye serve me so.
And wyll ye serve me so?
For my kindnes, thus to serve me so!

XI.

IN PRAISE OF THE JOYFUL LIFE OF A BACHELOR.

From sir J. Hawkins's History of Music.

The bachelor most joyfullye,
　In pleasant plight doth pass his daies,
Good fellowshipp and companie
　He doth maintaine and kepe alwaie[s].

With damsells brave he maye well goe,
The maried man cannot doe so,
If he be merie and toy with any,
　His wife will frowne, and words geve manye:
Her yellow hose she strait will put on,
So that the married man dare not displease his wife
　　Joane.

XII.

MY SWETE SWETYNG.

From the same work.

[My swetyng] is so proper and pure,
Full stedfast, stabill and demure,
There is none such, ye may be sure,
      As my swete sweting.

In all thys world, as thynketh me,
Is none so plesaunt to my eye,
That I am glad soo ofte to see,
      As my swete swetyng.

When I behold my swetyng swete,
Her face, her hands, her minion fete,
They seme to me there is none so mete,
      As my swete swetyng.

Above all other prayse must I,
And love my pretty pygsnye,
For none I fynd soo womanly
      As my swete swetyng.

XIII.

MUTUAL AFFECTION.

From a MS. of the Harleian collection (No. 3362.)

My joye it is from her to here,
  Whom that my mynd ys ever to see,
And to my hart she ys most nere,
  For I love hur and she lovyth me.

Of deuty nedes I múst hur love,
  Which hath my hart so stedfastly,
Therfore my hart shall not remove,
  But styll love hur whyle she lovyth me.

Both love for love and hart for hart,
  Which hath my hart so stedfastly,   10
Ther ys no payne may me convert,
  For I love hur and she lovyth me.

Chryst wolt the fuger of hur swete face
  Were pyctored wher ever I ' be,'
Yn every hall, from place to place,
  For I love hur and she lovyth me *.

V. 14. dwell.

* In mr. Ritsons transcript of this song, for the present edition, the 7th and 11th verses are transposed, and the concluding stanza, of the manuscript copy, omitted. *Ed.*

XIV.

THE PROFFERED SERVICES OF AFFECTION.

Mɪ hart, my mynde and my hole poure,
   My servyce trew, wyth all my myght,
On lond or see, in storme and shour,
   I geve to you, be day and nyght,
   And eke my body for to fyght,
My goods, also, be at your plesur,
Take me, and myne, as your owne tresure.

When your wyll is, be nyght or day,
   To ryde or go I wyll be prest,
And not refuse that I do may   10
   To perysh the hart wythin my brest
   Adversant trobles at your request
Shall me not dere, but to be pleasure,
Take me and myn, as your owne tresure.

Yf ye fare well, great myrth I make,
   Yf you mysfare, the contrary,
My grefe doth grow, my myrth doth slake,
   And redi I am strayt for to dye.
   As ye do fare, evyn so fare I;
Your wo my payn, your joy my plesur,   20
Take me and myne, as your owne treasure.

Yow for to please, it ys my mynd,
  And you to serve my wyll yt ys;
What shuld I more thus waste my wynd,
  I have nothyng that you can myse,
  Nor ought can do wyth my servyce:
And shal be [wholely] at youer pleasure,
Take me and myne, as youre own treasure.

Ancient Songs and Ballads.

CLASS IV.

COMPRISING

THE REIGNS OF EDWARD VI., QUEEN MARY, AND QUEEN ELIZABETH.

I.

THE DYING MAIDENS COMPLAINT.

From MSS. Sloan. No. 1584.

GREVUS ys my sorowe,
Both evyne and moro,
Unto myselffe alone,
Thus do I make my mowne,
That unkyndnes haith kyllyd me,
   And putt me to this peyne,
Alas! what remedy
   That I cannot refreyne!

Whan other men doyth sleype,
Thene do I syght and weype,   10
All 'ragin' in my bed,
As one for paynes neyre ded;
That unkyndnes have kyllyd me,
   And putt me to this payne,
Alas! what remedy
   That I cannott refreyne!

My harte ytt have no reste,
But styll wyth peynes oppreste,
And yett of all my smart,
Ytt grevith moste my harte,   20

[*V.* 11. ragins.]

That unkyndnes shuld kyll me,
   And putt me to this payne,
Alas! what remedy
   That I cannott refreyne!

Wo worth trust untrusty!
Wo worth love 'unlovely'!
Wo worth hape unblamyd!
Wo worth fautt unnamyd!
Thus unkyndly to kyll me,
   And putt me to this payn!   30
Now alas! what remedy
   That I cannott refrayne!

Alas! I lyve to-longe,
My paynes be so stronge,
For comforth have I none,
God wott I wold fayne be gone;
For unkyndnes haith kyllyd me,
   And putt me to this payne,
Alas! what remedy
   That I cannott refreyne.   40

Iff ony wyght be here
That byeth love so dere
Come nere, lye downe by me,
And weype for company,

      [*V.* 26. unlovyd.]

For unkyndnes haith kyllyd me,
   And putt me to this payne,
Alas! what remedy
   That I cannott refrayne.

My foes, whiche love me nott,
Bevayle my deth, I wott,   50
And he that love me beste
Hymeselfe my deth haith dreste;
What unkyndnes shuld kyle me,
   If this ware nott my payne,
Alas! what remedy
   That I cannott refreyne!

My last wyll here I make,
To god my soule I betake,
And my wrechyd body,
As erth, in a hole to lye: 60
For unkyndnes to kyle me,
   And putt me to this payne,
Alas! what remedy
   That I cannot refreyne!

O harte, I the bequyeth
To hyme that is my deth,
Yff that no harte haith he
My harte his schal be;
Thought unkyndnes haith kyllyd me,
   And putt me to this payne,   70
Yett, yf my body dyè,
   My hertt cannott refrayne.

Placebo, dilexi,
Com weype this obsequye,
My mowrnarus, dolfully,
Com weype this psalmody,
Of unkyndnes haith kyllyd me,
   And putt me to this payne,
Behold this wrechid body,
   That your unkyndnes haith slayne.

Now I besych all ye,
Namely, that lovers be,
My love my deth forgyve,
And soffer hyme to lyve;
Thought unkyndnes haith kyllyd me,
   And putt me to this payne,
Yett haid I rether dye
   For his sake ons agayne.

My tombe ytt schal be blewe,
In tokyne that I was trewe;
To bringe my love from doute,
Itt shal be wryttynge abowtte
That unkyndnes haith kyllyd me,
   And putt me to this payne:
Behold this wrechid body
   That your unkyndnes haith slayne!

O lady, lerne by me,
Sley nott love wylfully,
For fer love waxyth denty.

Unkyndnes to kyle me,
  Or putt love to this payne 100
I ware better dye
  For loves sake agayne.

Grevus is my soro,
But deth ys my boro,
For to myselfe alone
Thus do I make my mone,
That unkyndnes haith kyllyd me,
  And passyd is my payne.
Prey for this ded body, 110
  That your unkyndnes haith slayne.

II.

TYE THE MARE, TOM BOY.

BY WILLIAM BYRD.

This very old and once very favourite and popular song is given from a MS. collection of Old Songs, &c. formerly used in and about the bishoprick of Durham, sometime the property of James Mickleton, esquire, and now in the Harleian library (No. 7578). The music, by "Robert Johnson," a well known composer of Henry the 8th time, is a continued harmony from the beginning to the end.

  The following song is particularly alluded to in the "pleasing merrie Interlude" of "Tom Tyler and his wyfe," first printed in 1578? And in Ames's *Typographical Antiquities* (p. 308) is "A ballet, declaringe the fal of the whore of Babylone, intituled, *Tye thy mare Tom-boye*, &c." which, though for what reason does not appear, he has placed under the year 1547.

According to Wood, John Plough became a zealous minister in the time of king Edward the sixth, but, flying beyond sea in queen Marys reign, wrote against one William Keth, an exile at Frankfort, in that reign; who, according to Tanner, is the writer of this ballad.

Ty the mare, Tom boy, ty the mare, Tom boy,
 Lest she stray
 From the awaye,
Now ty the mare, Tom boy.

The mare is so mynyone,
 So smoth and so smikere,
That, in myne apynion,
 Ther is nott a trykere
From hence to Avynion,
 Yf she ware nott a kyckere,   10
Att ned, by sentt Nynyon,
 I knowe nott a quycker.
Now, ty the mar, Tom boy, &c.

Gyll, now to name her,
 A mare of good mold,
She wold be mayd tamer,
 Yff 'tame her' whoo could,
' Her ' dame was a framer,
 To ryd 'her' who shuld,
No labur could lame ' her,'   20
 To gallape whille they wolde.
Now, ty the mare, Tom boy, &c.

[*V.* 17. tamer.]

Because thou dost lyke her,
   And lyst nott to chang her,
I wold she were meker,
   And be no more a ranger;
But she is a striker,
   And therin her danger,
For hym that shalle kepe her
   At racke and att manger.   30
Now, ty the mare, Tom boy, &c.

At larg yf thou lett her,
   Thay seke and can nott fynd her,
Yett wer thou much better
   In trammells to bynd her;
A loock and a fetter
   Befor and behynd her,
At lyver to sett her,
   Wher thou lyst to asyne her.
Now, ty the mare, Tom boy, &c.   40

The trimer thou tyuer her,
   To show her a starrer,
The mo wille desyer her,
   And, therfor, bewar her;
For whoo that may hyer her
   To ryd wille nott spar her,
But no man can tyer her,
   Whille towe legges may bear her.
[Now,] ty the mare, Tom boy, &c.

Yf hunger dysease her, 50
   'Then' must thou be watching
With hard meatt to pleas her,
   That she may be catchyng
A morsell to dasse her,
   Therat to be snaching;
Such baytt shall apease her,
   Yf thou mayk no patching.
Now, ty the mar, Tom boy, &c.

To glosse or to glaver,
   I will for no medyng, 60
But yffe thou wilt have her
   All tymes at thy nedyng.
Lett her nott tayk saver
   At 'other' mens fedyng,
For, then, will they crave her
   Because of her bredyng.
Now, ty the mar, &c.

A fooll of that fylly,
   That ware lyke her mother,
From Seland to Sylley 70
   Ware nott such another:
No mor of her will I
   Speak one word nor other,
But make much of Gylly,
   I pray the, Tom, brother.
Nowe, tye the mar, Tom boy, &c.

       [*V.* 64. others.]

III.

IN DISPRAISE OF WOMEN.

From the same MS. Where it is attended with musical notes, but as " ther laketh all the other parts," these are not copied. At the end is, *finis q. mr. Heath;* but whether he were author, or composer, or both, or neither, is altogether uncertain.

THESE women all,
Both great and small,
 Ar wavering to and fro,
Now her, now ther,
Now every wher:—
 But I will nott say so.

They love to range,
Ther myndes 'do' chaunge;
 And maks ther 'frynd' ther foo;
As lovers trewe   10
Eche daye they chewse new:—
 But I will nott say so.

They laughe, they smylle,
They do begyle,
 As dyce that men 'do' throwe;
Who useth them 'mych'
Shall never be ryche:—
 But I will not say so.

Summe hot, sum cold,
Ther is no hold,   20
  But as the wynd doth blowe;
When all is done,
They chaung lyke the moone:—
  But I will not say so.

So thus one and other
Takith after ther mother,
  As 'cocke' by kind doth crowe.
My song is ended,
The beste may be amended:—
  But I will nott say so.   30

IV.

THE DISCONTENTED HUSBAND.

From a MS. in the Cotton library (Vespasian, A. xxv.)

THE man ys blest
That lyves in rest,
And so can keep him stylle;
  And he is 'accurst'
  That was the first
That gave hys wyff her wyll.

[*V.* 4. a coruste.]

What paine and gr[i]eff
  Without relieff
Shall we pore men sustayne
  Yff every Gyle   10
  Shall have her wyle,
And over us shall reigne!

  Then all our wyves,
  During ther lyves,
Wyll loke to do the same,
  And beare in hand,
  Yt ys as lande,
That goeth not from the name.

  There ys no man
  Whose wysdome canne   20
Reforme a wylfull wyff,
  But onely god
  Who maide the rod
For our unthryfty lyffe.

  Let us, therefor,
  Crye owt and rore,
And make to god request,
  That he redresse
  This wilfulnes,
And set our hartes at rest.   30

  Wherefor, good wyves,
  Amende your lyves,

And we wyll do the same;
And kepe not style
That nought ye wyle
That haith so evell a name.

V.

CAPTAIN CAR.

The elegant editor of the " Reliques of Ancient English Poetry" has inserted in that collection a Scotish ballad, entitled " Edom o' Gordon," printed at Glasgow in 1755; but " improved, and enlarged with several fine stanzas, recovered from a fragment of the same ballad in 'his' folio MS." and by him " clothed in the Scotish orthography and idiom." Of the ballad to which the above fragment appears to have belonged, the reader is here presented with an entire ancient copy, the undoubted original of the Scotish ballad, and one of the few specimens now extant of the genuine proper Old English Ballad, as composed—not by a Grub-street author for the stalls of London, but—to be chanted up and down the kingdom by the wandering minstrels of " the North Countrie." This curiosity is preserved in a miscellaneous collection in the Cotton Library, marked Vespasian, A. xxv. At the top of the original stands the word *Jhus* (Jesus), and at the end is *Finis ꝑ me Willm̄ Asheton Cleric̄u:* the name and quality, we may presume, of the original author. The MS. having received numerous alterations or corrections, all or most of which are evidently for the better, they are here adopted as part of the text.

The historical fact which gave occasion to, and forms the subject of, the following ballad, and which happened in the year 1571, may be found both in archbishop Spotswoods History (an extract of which is given in the later editions of Percy), and in the Memoirs published by Crawford of Drumsoy.

Dr. Percy is of opinion, that " from the different titles of this ballad the old strolling bards or minstrels made no scruple of changing the names of the personages they introduced, to humour the hearers." If such a practice ever prevailed, it is very certain that the present ballad affords no instance of it, as in fact CAR (or, according to the Scotish orthography, KER) was actually sent with a party by sir ADAM GORDON, who commanded for the Queen, as deputy to his brother the earl of Huntley, to summon the castle of Towy or Tavoy (here called Crecrynbroghe), belonging to Alexander Forbes (here called the lord Hamleton), and which, instead of surrendering, was resolutely defended by his lady, who gave Car very injurious language. Now though it does not appear that his barbarity—for he actually set fire to the castle, and burnt therein the lady and her whole family, to the amount in all of thirty-seven persons—was authorised (if indeed it could have been authorised) by any previous orders, yet as he was never called to any account for it, the infamy of the transaction naturally extended to Gordon, who from the superiority of his station might even be considered as the greater criminal; and as he was, at the same time, better known, his name was naturally substituted by the Scotish minstrels for that of his subordinate officer.

IT befell at martynmas,
 When wether waxed colde,
Captaine Care saide to his men,
 We must go take a holde.

" Haille, master, and wether you will,
 And wether ye like it best."
" To the castle of Crecrynbroghe,
 And there we will take our reste."

" I knowe wher is a gay castle,
 Is build of lyme and stone,
Within ' there ' is a gay ladie,
 Her lord is ryd from hom."

The ladie lend on her castle-walle,
    She loked upp and downe,
There was she ware of an host of men,
    Come riding to the towne.

" Com yow hether, my meri men all,
    And look what I do see;
Yonder is ther an host of men,
    I musen who they bee."   20

She thought he had been her own wed lord,
    That had comd riding home;
Then was it traitour captaine Care,
    The lord of Ester-towne.

They were no soner at supper sett,
    Then after said the grace,
Or captaine Care and all his men
    Wer lighte aboute the place.

" Gyve over thi howsse, thou lady gay,
    And I will make the a bande,   30
To-nighte thoust ly wythin my arm[es],
    To-morrowe thou shall ere my lan[de]."

Then bespacke the eldest sonne,
    That was both whitt and redde,
O mother dere, geve over your howsse,
    Or elles we shal be deade.

I will not geve over my hoūs, she saithe,
    Not for feare of my lyffe,
It shal be talked throughout the land
    The slaughter of a wyffe.   40

" Fetche me my pestilett,
    And charge me my gonne,
That I may shott at ' the ' bloddy butcher,
    The lord of Easter-towne."

She styfly stod on her castle-wall,
    And lett the pellettes flee,
She myst the blody bucher,
    And slew other three.

" I will not geve over my hous," she saithe,
    " Netheir for lord nor lowne,   50
Nor yet for traitour captaine Care,
    The lord of Easter-towne.

I desire of captaine Care,
    And all his bloddye band,
That he would save my eldest sonne,
    The eare of all my lande."

" Lap him in a shete," he sayth,
    " And let him downe to me,
And I shall take him in my armes,
    His waran wyll I be."   60

The captayne sayd unto himselfe,
    Wyth sped before the rest:
He cut his tonge out of his head,
    His hart out of his brest.

He lapt them in a handkerchef,
    And knet it of knotes three,
And cast them over the castell-wall
    At that gay ladye.

" Fye upon thee, captayne Care,
    And all thy bloddy band,   70
For thou hast slayne my eldest sonne,
    The ayre of all my land."

Then bespake the yongest sonn,
    That sat on the nurses knee,
Sayth, mother gay, geve over your house,
    [The smoke] it smoldereth me.

I wold geve my gold, she saith,
    And so I wolde my fee,
For a blaste of the ' western ' wind
    To dryve the smoke from thee.   80

" Fy upon the, John Hamleton,
    That ever I paid the hyre,
For thou hast broken my castle-wall,
    And kyndled in ' it ' fyre."

            [*V*. 79. wesleyn.]
            [*V*. 84. thee.]

The lady gate to her close parlèr,
  The fire fell aboute her head,
She toke up her children thre,
  'Seth, babes, we are all dead.

Then bespake the hye stewàrd,
  That is of hye degree,   90
Saith, Ladie gay, you are no 'bote'
  Wethere ye fighte or flee.

Lord Hamleton dremd in his dreame,
  In Carvall where he laye,
His halle 'was' all of fyre,
  His ladie slayne or daye.

" Busk and bowne, my mery men all,
  Even and go ye with me,
For I 'dremd' that my hall was [all] on fyre,
  My lady slayne or day."   100

He buskt him and bownd hym,
  'All' like a worthi knighte,
And when he saw his hall burning,
  His harte was no dele lighte.

He sett a trumpett till his mouth,
  He blew as it plesd his grace,
Twenty score of Hamletons
  Was light aboute the place.

[*V*. 102. and.]

"Had I knowne asmuch yesternighte
  As I do to-daye,   110
Captaine Care and all his men
  Should not have gone so quite [awaye].

Fye upon the, captaine Care,
  And all thy blody 'bande,'
Thou hast slayne my lady gaye;
  More worth 'than' all thy lande."

Yf thou had ought eny ill will, he saith,
  Thou shoulde have taken my lyffe,
And have saved my children thre,
  All and my lovesome wyffe.   120

VI.

A MERY BALLET OF THE HATHORNE TRE,

————"To be songe after Donkin Dargeson," from the same MS. This tune, whatever it was, appears to have been in use till after the Restoration. In a volume of old ballads in the possession of John Baynes, esq., is one "to the tune of Dargeson."

It was a maide of my countrè,
As she came by a hathorne-tre,
As full of flowers as might be seen,
'She' mervel'd to se the tre so grene.

[*V.* 116. then.]
[*V.* 4. Se.]

At last she asked of this tre,
Howe came this freshnes unto the,
And every branche so faire and cleane?
I mervaile that you growe so grene.

The tre 'made' answere by and by,
I have good causse to growe triumphantly, 10
The swetest dew that ever be sene
Doth fall on me to kepe me grene.

Yea, quoth the maid, but where you growe,
You stande at hande for every blowe,
Of every man for to be seen,
I mervaile that you growe so grene.

"Though many one take flowers from me,
And manye a branche out of my tre,
I have suche store they wyll not be sene, 19
For more and more my 'twegges' growe grene."

"But howe and they chaunce to cut the downe,
And carry thie braunches into the towne?
Then will they never no more be sene
To growe againe so freshe and grene."

"Thoughe that you do, yt ys no boote,
Althoughe they cut me to the roote,
Next yere againe I will be sene
To bude my branches freshe and grene:

[*V.* 20. twedges.]

And you, faire maide, canne not do so,
For yf you let youre maid-hode goe, 30
Then will yt never no more be sene,
As I with my braunches can growe grene."

The maide, wyth that, beganne to blushe,
And turned her from the hathorne-bushe,
She though[t]e herselffe so faire and clene,
Her bewtie styll would ever growe grene.

Whan that she harde this marvelous dowbte,
She wandered styll then all aboute,
Suspecting still what she would wene,
Her maid-heade lost would never be seen. 40

Wyth many a sighe, she went her waye,
To se howe she made herselff so gay,
To walke, to se, and to be sene,
And so out-faced the hathorne-grene.

Besides all that, yt put her in feare,
To talke with companye anye where,
For feare to losse the thinge that shuld be sene
To growe as were the hathorne-grene.

But, after this, never could I 'hear,'
Of this faire mayden any where, 50
That ever she was in forest sene,
To talke againe of the hathorne-grene.

[*V*. 49. here.]

VII.

THE LAMENTATION OF GEORGE MANNINGTON,

Written an hour before he suffered at Cambridge-castle, 1576: to the tune of *Labundula shott.*

In *Eastward hoe*, by Jonson, Chapman, and Marston, Quicksilver the apprentice is introduced, as a prisoner in the Counter, reading some verses, which he calls his *Repentance;* he then says,

"*Quick.* I writ it when my spirits were oppress'd.
St. Petro. Ay, I 'll be sworn for you, Francis.
Quick. It is in imitation of *Mannington's;* he that was hang'd at Cambridge, that cut off the horse's head at a blow.
Friend. So, sir.
Quick. To the tune of, *I wail in woe, I plunge in pain.*"
After repeating some of his poem, he proceeds in this manner:
"*Quick.* The stanza now following alludes to the story of *Mannington*, from whence I took my project for my invention.
Friend. Pray you go on, sir.
Quick. O *Mannington*, thy stories shew,
 Thou cutt'st a horse head off at a blow;
 But I confess I have not the force,
 For to cut off the head of a horse,
 Yet I desire this grace to win,
 That I may cut off the horse head of sin:
 And leave his body in the dust
 Of sin's highway, and bogs of lust;
 Whereby I may take virtue's purse,
 And live with her for better, for worse."

In the books of the Stationers company is the following entry, "7 November, 1576, licensed unto him (*i. e.* Richard Jones), a "ballad, intituled, A woeful Ballad, made by *mr. George Man-* "*nynton*, an hour before he suffered at Cambridge-castell." See

Dodsleys Collection [of Old Plays], Vol. iv. p. 294, 296. and Vol. xii. p. 394.

This ballad is given, and the above information extracted, from the Gentlemans Magazine for January, 1781; where the former is said, by the person who communicates it, under the signature of R. C., to be "written in a neat but at present not very legible hand, on a blank leaf in an old History of England;" the date 1582 appearing, in a different hand, on the opposite page.

This ballad is inserted in Robinsons "Handefull of pleasant delites," 1584, under the title of "A sorrowfull sonet, made by M. George Mannington at Cambridge-castle, to the tune of *Labundala Shot.*"

It would seem from a passage in Taylors *Navy of land ships*, that the tune was frequently danced to. See Steevens's *Shakspeare*, 1793, xiv. 369.

    I WAYLE in woe, I plundge in payne,
With sorrowing sobbes I do complayne,
With wallowing waves I wishe to dye,
I languishe sore here as I lye;
In feare I faynte, in hope I houlde,
With ruth I runne*, I was 'too' boulde,
As lucklesse lot assigned me,
In dangerous dale of destinie,
Hope bids me smyle, feare bids me weepe,
Such care my sillye soule doth keepe.   10

Yet too too late I do repent
The wicked wayes that I have spent,
The rechlesse care of carelesse kynde,
Which hath bewitched my wofull mynde:
Such is the chance, such is the state,
Of them that trust 'too' much to fate.

    * i. e. My eyes overflow with sorrow.

No bragging boaste of gentell bloudde,
What so it be, can do me good;
No witt, no strengthe, no bewties hewe,
What so it be, can death eschewe.　　20

The dysmall day hath had his will,
And justice seekes my lyfe to spill,
Revendgement craves by rigorous lawe,
Whereof I litell stood in awe,
The dolefull dumpes to end this lyfe
Bedeckt with care and worldly stryfe;
The frowning judge hath geven his dome,
O gentell death thou art welcome!
The losse of life I do not feare,
Then welcome death the end of care.　　30

My frendes and parents, 'where' you be,
Full litell do you thinke on me,
My mother mylde, and dame so deare,
Your loving chylde lyeth fettered 'here.'
Would god I had (I wish 'too' late)
Bene borne and 'bred' of meaner state!
Or els, would god my rechlesse eare
Had bene obedient for to heare
Your sage advyse and counsell trewe!
But, in the lord, parents, adue!　　40

You valyant hartes of youthfull trayne,
Which heare my heavie harte complayne,

[*V*. 31. wheresoever.]　　[*V*. 34. heare.]
[*V*. 36. bread.]

A good example take by me,
Which knue the kace 'wheree'er' you be
Trust not 'too' much to Bilboe-blade,
Nor yet to fortunes fickle trade;
Hoyste not your 'sayles' no more in wynde,
Leste that some rocke you chance to fynde,
Or else be dryven to Lybia land
Whereas the barke may sinke in sande.   50

You students all that present be
To viewe my fatall destenie,
Would god I could requyte your payne
Wherein you labour, 'though' in vayne.
If mightie Jove would thinke it good
To spare my lyfe and vytall bloud,
In this your proffered curtesie
I would remayne most stedfastly
Your servant true in deed and word:
But welcome death as pleaseth the lord.   60

'Yea,' welcome death, the ende of woe!
And farewell lyfe, my fatall foe!
'Yea,' welcome death, the end of stryfe!
Adue the care of mortall lyfe!
For, though this lyfe do flitt away,
In heaven I hope to lyve for aye;
A place of joye and perfect rest,
Which Christ hath purchased for the best:
Till that we meet in heaven most high'st,
Adue, farewell, in Jhesus Christ!   70

[*V.* 44. wheresoever.]   [*V.* 47. seales.]
[*V.* 54. although.]   [*VV.* 61. 63. ye.]

VIII.

THE PRAISE OF A COUNTRY-MANS LIFE,

BY JOHN CHALKHILL, ESQ.

"an acquaintant and friend of Edmund Spenser."

From Izaak Waltons "Compleat Angler." Lond. 1653. 8vo. Mr. Chalkhill is better known as the author of Thealma and Clearchus; but the time of his birth or death has not been discovered.

OH, the sweet contentment
   The country-man doth find,
High trolollie, lollie, loe, high trolollie, lee,
That quiet contemplation,
   Possesseth all my mind:
Then, care away, and wend along with me.

For courts are full of flattery,
   As hath too oft been 'try'd'
High trolollie, lollie, loe, high trolollie, lee,
The city full of wantonness,   10
   And both are full of pride:
Then, care away, and wend along with me.

But, oh the honest country-man
   Speaks truly from his heart,
High trolollie, lollie, loe, high trolollie, lee.
His pride is in his tillage,
   His horses and his cart:
Then, care away, and wend along with me.

Our clothing is good sheep-skins,
    Gray russet for our wives,   20
High trolollie, lollie, loe, high trolollie, lee,
'Tis warmth and not gay clothing
    That doth prolong our lives:
Then, care away, and wend along with me.

The ploughman, though he labor hard,
    Yet, on the holy-day,
High trolollie, lollie, loe, high trolollie, lee,
No emperor so merrily
    Does pass his time away:
Then, care away, and wend along with me.   30

To recompence our tillage
    The heavens afford us showrs;
High trolollie, lollie, loe, high trolollie, lee.
And for our sweet refreshments
    The earth affords us bowers:
Then, care away, and wend along with me.

The cuckoe and the nightingale
    Full merrily do sing,
High trolollie, lollie, loe, high trolollie, lee.
And, with their pleasant roundelayes,   40
    Bid welcome to the spring:
Then, care away, and wend along with me.

This is not half the happiness
    The country-man injoyes;

High trolollie, lollie, loe, high trolollie, lee,
Though others think they have as much,
  Yet he that sayes so lies:
Then, come away, turn count[r]y-man with me.

IX.

THE THREE RAVENS.

A DIRGE.

From Ravenscrofts " Melismata. Musical Phansies. Fitting the Cittie, and Countrey Humours. To 3, 4, and 5 voyces. Lond. 1611." 4to; where it is inserted under the head of " Country Pastimes." This ballad is much older, not only than the date of the book, but than most of the other pieces contained in it.
The immediately following article is " The marriage of the frogge and the mouse." The mean, tenor, and bass parts are only for the chorus or burthen.

THERE were three ravens sat on a tree,
  Downe, a downe, hay down, hay downe,
There were three ravens sat on a tree,
  With a downe,
There were three ravens sat on a tre,
They were as blacke as they might be,
  With a downe, derrie, derrie, derrie, downe, downe.

The one of them said to his 'make,'
Where shall we our breakefast take?

[*V.* 8. mate.]

"Downe in yonder greene field,   10
There lies a knight slain under his shield.

His hounds they lie downe at his feete,
So well they their master keepe.

His haukes they flie so eagerly,
There's no fowle dare him come nie."

Downe there comes a fallow doe,
As great with yong as she might goe.

She lift up his bloudy hed,
And kist his wounds that were so red.

She got him up upon her backe,   20
And carried him to earthen lake.

She buried him before the prime,
She was dead herselfe ere even-song time.

God send every gentleman
Such haukes, such hounds, and such a leman.

X.

THE TOO COURTEOUS KNIGHT.

From "Deuteromelia: or the Second part of Musicks melodie, or melodious Musicke. Of pleasant Roundelaies; K. H. [King Henrys] mirth or Freemens Songs, and such delightful Catches. Lond. 1609." 4to. This is a sequel to "Pammelia," a collection

of a similar nature, published in the same year; and, like it, "contains a great number of fine vocal compositions of very great antiquity." See Hawkinses *Hist. Music*, vol. iv. p. 18.
This song is in the first volume of some editions, the third in others, of Durfeys *Pills to purge Melancholy;* and in a different volume is a modernised copy of it, with considerable variations, beginning—

" There was a knight, and he was young."

Bp. Percy found the subject worthy of his best improvements; see *Reliques*, vol. ii. p. 341.
In Major Pearsons collection of Old Ballads is a different copy, intitled, " The Politick Maid," beginning—

" There was a knight was wine dronke."

YONDER comes a courteous knight,
    Lustely raking over the lay,
He was well ware of a bonny lasse,
    As she came wandering over the way.
Then she sang *Downe a downe, hey downe derry.*

Jove you speed, fayre lady, he said,
    Among the leaves that be so greene;
If I were a king and wore a crowne,
    Full soone, faire lady, shouldst thou be a queen.
Then she sang, *Downe,* &c.   10

Also Jove save you faire lady,
    Among the roses that be so red;
If I have not my will of you,
    Full soone faire lady shall I be dead.
Then she sang, &c.

Then he lookt East, then hee lookt West,
   Hee lookt North, so did he South;
He could not finde a privy place,
   For all lay in the divels mouth.
Than she sang, &c.   20

If you will carry me, gentle sir,
   A mayde unto my fathers hall,
Then you shall have your will of me,
   Under purple and under paule.
Than she sang, &c.

He set her up upon a steed,
   And him selfe upon another:
And all the day he rode her by,
   As though they had been sister and brother.
Then she sang, &c.   30

When she came to her fathers hall,
   It was well walled round about;
She yode in at the wicket gate
   And shut the foure ear'd foole without.
Then she sang, &c.

You had me (quoth she) abroad in the field,
   Among the corne, amidst the hay;
Where you might had your will of mee,
   For, in good faith sir, I never said nay.
Then she sang, &c.   40

Ye had me also amid the field,
  Among the rushes that were so browne;
Where you might had your will of me,
  But you had not the face to lay me downe.
Then she sang, &c.

He pulled out his nut-browne sword,
  And wipt the rust off with his sleeve;
And said, Joves curse come to his heart,
  That any woman would believe.
Then she sang, &c.

XI.

JOHN DORY.

This celebrated old ballad, which, could due proof be obtained of its real antiquity, would, in all probability, be found to belong to the preceding, or, possibly, even to an anterior, class, is given from the publication last described, where it is inserted among the " Freemens songs of 3 voices." This was the favourite performance of the English Minstrels so lately as the reign of King Charles II. "Hunger," says Bp. Earle in his character of a poor Fiddler, "is the greatest pain he takes, except a broken head sometimes, and the labouring JOHN DORY:" and Dryden, in one of his lampoons, refers to it as to the most hackneyed thing of the time:

" But Sunderland, Godolphin, Lory,
  These will appear such chits in story,
    'Twill turn all politics to jests,
  TO BE REPEATED LIKE *JOHN DORY*,
    WHEN FIDLERS SING AT FEASTS."

In the *Chances,* by Fletcher, first printed in 1647, but written long before, the author having died in 1625, old Antonio, when under the hands of the surgeon, who asks if indulgence in allowing music will please, says,

"———Yes; and let 'em sing
JOHN DORRIE.
2 *Gent.* 'Tis too long.
Ant. I'll have JOHN DORRIE!
For to that warlike tune I will be open'd."

The "Song of JOHN DORRIE" is accordingly supposed to be sung, for which he orders the musicians ten shillings. It is likewise alluded to in the *Knight of the Burning Pestle*, Act II., and still more circumstantially by the facetious Bp. Corbett, who tells us, that he

"——— to PARIS rode along,
Much like JOHN DORY in the SONG,
UPON AN HOLY TIDE.
' He' on AN AMBLING NAG did get, &c."

Carew, in his *Survey of Cornwall*, London, 1602, 4to. fo. 135, speaking of the town and inhabitants of Fowey, has the following words: "Moreover the prowesse of one Nicholas, sonne to a widdow neere Foy, is deskanted upon in an old three mans song, namely, how he fought bravely at sea, with John Dory (a Genowey, as I conjecture), set forth by John the French king, and (after much bloudshed on both sides) tooke, and slew him, in revenge of the great ravine and crueltie, which he had fore committed, upon the Englishmens goods and bodies." It is scarcely worth mentioning that the only king of France of the name of John (excepting, indeed, a posthumous son of Lewis Hutin, who lived only eight days) was taken prisoner at the battle of Poictiers, and died in the Savoy, anno 1364.

In the epilogue to a dramatic performance, intitled, "The empress of Morocco, a farce," 1674, 4to. "the most renowned and melodious song of JOHN DORY" is "heard as it were in the air sung in parts by spirits to raise the expectation, and charm the audience with thoughts sublime, and worthy of the heroick scene which follows," being apparently designed as a burlesque of the witch-scene in sir W. Davenants alteration of Macbeth.

As it fell on a holy-day,
   And upon ' a ' holy-tide-a,
John Dory bought him an ambling nag,
   To Paris for to ride-a:

And, when John Dory to Paris was come,
   A little before the gate-a,
John Dory was fitted, the porter was witted,
   To let him in thereat-a.

The first man, that John Dory did meet,
   Was good king John of France-a;   10
John Dory could well of his courtesie,
   But fell downe in a trance-a:

" A pardon, a pardon, my liege and my king,
   For my merie men and for me-a;
And all the churles in merie Englànd,
   Ile bring them all bound to thee-a."

And Nicholl was then a Cornish man,
   A little beside Bohide-a;
And he mande forth a good blacke barke,
   With fiftie good oares on a side-a.   20

" Run up my boy unto the maine top,
   And looke what thou canst spie-a."
' Who ho! who ho! a goodly ship I do see,
   I trow it be John Dorỳ-a."

They hoist their sailes, both top and top,
   The meisseine and all was tride-a;
And every man stood to his lot,
   Whatever should betide-a.

The roring cannons then were plide,
   And dub-a-dub went the drumme-a;   30
The braying trumpets lowd they cride,
   To courage both all and some-a.

The grapling-hooks were brought at length,
   The browne bill and the sword-a;
John Dory at length, for all his strength,
   Was clapt fast under board-a.

XII.

THE SPRING-TIME.

BY WILLIAM SHAKSPEARE.

———is sung by two pages in the comedy of "As you like it;" of which play there is no earlier edition than the folio in 1623; whence it is here given: but the stanzas being evidently misplaced (that which is now the last stanza being there the second), they are here transposed according to the regulation of the ingenious dr. Thirlby.

"As you like it" appears to have been entered at Stationers-hall, Aug. 4, 1600.

It was a lover and his lass,
   With a hey and a ho and a hey nonino,
That o'er the green corn-field did pass,
      In the spring-time,
      The onely pretty 'ring'-time,
      When birds do sing
      Hey ding a ding ding;
      Sweet lovers love the spring.

Between the acres of the rye,
  With a hey and a ho and a hey nonino,
These pretty country-folks would lye·
    In the spring time,
      &c.

The carol they began that hour,
  With a hey and a ho and a hey nonino,
How, that life was but a flower,
    In the spring-time,
      &c.

And, therefore, take the present time,
  With a hey and a ho and a hey nonino,
For love is crowned with the prime,
    In the spring-time.
      &c.

XIII.

THE POWER OF MUSIC.

BY THE SAME.

From the " History of King Henry VIII.," in which it appears to have been originally sung to the lute by one of Queen Catharines female attendants. This play, though not printed before 1623, contains intrinsic evidence of having been finished before the death of queen Elizabeth.

These stanzas were set to music, for three voices, by Matthew Locke, See Playfords *Catch that catch can, or Musical Companion,* 1667.

ORPHEUS, with his lute, made trees
And the mountaine-tops, that freeze,
  Bow themselves, when he did sing;
To his musicke, plants, and flowers,
Ever sprung; as sunne and showers
  There had made a lasting spring.

Every thing, that heard him play,
Even the billowes of the sea,
  Hung their heads, and then lay by
In sweet musicke is such art;
Killing care and griefe of heart
  Fall asleepe, or, hearing, dye.

XIV.

HARK! HARK! THE LARK.

BY THE SAME.

—is sung by Clotens musicians under Imogens window, in " Cymbeline," act ii. scene 3. We are entirely ignorant of the nature of the original music, but every one is acquainted with the beautiful glee composed by dr. Cooke.

HARK! hark! the lark at heavens gate ' sing,'
  And Phœbus gins arise,
His steeds to water at ' that spring '
  On chalic'd flowers that lies:

And winking Mary-buds begin,
  To ope their golden eyes;
With every thing that pretty 'bin:'
  " My lady sweet, arise!"

XV.

THE MOTHERS LULLABY.

From a MS. of James the Ists time. Bibl. Sloan. 1708.

My little sweete derlinge, my comforte and joye,
  Singe lullyby, lully,
In bewtie excellinge the princes of Troye,
  Singe lullaby, lully.

Nowe, sucke, childe, and sleepe, child, thy mothers
    sweete boye,
The gods blesse and keepe thee from cruell annoy,
Thy father, sweete infant, from mother ys gone,
And shee, in the woodes heere, with thee lefte alone.

To thee, little infant, why do I make mone,
  Singe lully, lully,
Sith thou canst not helpe mee to sighe nor to grone,
  Singe lully, lully, lully,
    Sweete baby, lullyby, sweete baby, lully, lully.

XVI.

THE GARLAND.

BY BEAUMONT OR FLETCHER.

This elegant little piece is found in " The Maids Tragedy," by Beaumont and Fletcher, first printed in 1619, where it is sung by Aspatia, being introduced by a short dialogue between her and Evadne.

> Lay a garland on my hearse
>   Of the dismal yew;
> Maidens, willow branches bear;
>   Say, I died true.
>
> My love was false, but I was firm
>   From my hour of birth:
> Upon my bury'd body lie
>   Lightly, gentle earth!

XVII.

THE JOVIAL TINKER.

" Dispersed through Shakespeare's plays are innumerable little fragments of ancient ballads, the entire copies of which could not be recovered. Many of these being of the most beautiful and pathetic simplicity, the editor was tempted to select some of them, and with a few supplemental stanzas to connect them together, and form them into a little TALE, which is here submitted to the readers candour.

' Two or three' small 'fragments' were taken from Beaumont and Fletcher."

It was a jovial tinker,
 All of the north countriè,
As he walk'd forth, along the way,
 He sung right merrily.

" The ousel-cock, so black of hue,
 With orange-tawny bill,
The throstle with his note so true,
 The wren with little quill:

The finch, the sparrow, and the lark,
 The plain-song cuckow grey, 10
Whose note full many a man doth mark,
 And dares not answer, Nay."

" Now, Christ thee save, thou jolly tinkèr,
 Now Christ thee save and see;
My true love hast thou chanc'd to meet,
 I pray thee, tell to me."

" And how should I know your true love,
 From another one?"
" O, by his slouched hat and staff,
 And by his clouted shoone; 20

But, chiefly, by his comely nose,
    That is so fair to see:
My bonny sweet Robin is all my joy,
    And ever more shall be."

" O, lady, your true love is false,
    Lady, he is untrue;
For he has got him another love,
    And quite forsaken you.

He set her on a milk-white steed
    And his self upon a grey;   30
He never turn'd his face again,
    But bore her quite away."

" And will he not come again?
    And will he not come again?"
" No, no, he is gone, and we'll cast away moan,
    For he never will come again.

But, shall we go mourn for that, my dear?
    The pale moon shines by night:
And, when we wander here and there,
    We then do go most right.   40

If tinkers may have leave to live,
    And bear the sow-skin budget,
Then my account I well may give,
    And in the stocks avouch it.

Jog on, jog on, the foot-path way,
    And merrily hent the stile-a;
A merry heart goes all the day,
    Your sad tires in a mile-a.

For, I the ballad will repeat,
    Which men full true shall find;   50
Your marriage comes by destiny,
    Your cuckow sings by kind."

" O heart! o heart! o heavy heart!
    Why sigh'st thou without breaking?
Because thou canst not ease thy smart,
    By friendship, nor by speaking?"

With that she sighed as she stood,
    And gave this sentence then,
Among nine bad, if one be good,
    There's yet one good in ten.   60

" Lady, what wilt thou do, lady?
    Lady, what would'st thou be?
Tell me thy mind, thy friend I'll prove,
    As, quickly, thou shalt see."

" I would not be a serving man,
    To carry the cloak-bag still;
Nor would I be a falconer,
    The greedy hawks to fill.

But I would be in a good house,
　And have a good master too;
And I would eat and drink the best,
　And no work would I do.

But I will cut my pretty green coat,
　A foot above my knee;
And I will clip my yellow locks,
　An inch below my eye.

And I will buy a little white horse,
　Thereon forth for to ride;
And I'll go seek my own true-love,
　Throughout the world so wide."

" Yet, stay thee, lady, turn again,
　And dry those weeping tears,
For, see, beneath this tinkers garb,
　Thy own true-love appears!"

" Now, farewell grief, and welcome joy,
　Once more unto my heart;
For, since I have found thee, lovely youth,
　We never more will part."

XVIII.

ROBIN LEND TO ME THY BOW.

A canon in the unison, for four voices, from "Pammelia. Musicks Miscellanie. Or, Mixed varietie of Pleasant Roundelayes, and delightfull Catches, of 3, 4, 5, 6, 7, 8, 9, 10, parts in one. Lond. 1609, 4to." That it was a popular song in the beginning of Queen Elizabeths reign appears from its being cited (amongst others) in a curious old musical piece, (MSS. Harl. 7578, before mentioned) containing the description and praises of the city of Durham, written about that time; but of which the corresponding parts are unfortunately lost. It is likewise quoted in "A very mery and pythie commedie, called The longer thou livest the more foole thou art." By W. Wager, London, 4to. b. l. n. d.

Now Robin lend to me thy bow,
  Sweet Robin lend to me thy bow,
For I must now a hunting with my lady goe,
  With my sweet lady goe.
   Now, *ut sup*.

And whither will thy lady goe?
  Sweet Wilkin tell it unto mee;
And thou shalt have my hawke, my hound, and eke
   my bow,
  To wait on thy lady.

My lady will to Uppingham*,
  To Uppingham forsooth will shee;
And I my selfe appointed for to be the man,
  To wait on my lady.

   * A market town in Rutlandshire.

Adieu, good Wilkin, all beshrewde,
    Thy hunting nothing pleaseth mee;
But yet beware thy babling hounds stray not abroad,
    For angring of thy lady.

My hounds shall be led in the line
    So well I can assure it thee;
Unlesse by view of straine some pursue I may finde,
    To please my sweet lady.   20

With that the lady shee came in,
    And wild them all for to agree;
For honest hunting never was accounted sinne,
    Nor never shall for mèe.

XIX.

FLODDON FIELD.

BY THOMAS DELONEY.

The battle of Floddon, in Northumberland, was fought the 9th of September, 1513, being the fifth year of King Henry the 8th (who, with a great army, was then before Tcrouen in France) between Thomas Howard, earl of Surrey, commander-in-chief of the English forces, and James the 4th, king of Scots, with an inferior army of 15,000 men, who were entirely routed with great slaughter, their heroic sovereign being left dead upon the field.

The relation of this signal victory and defeat has been the subject of as much rejoicing with the poets of England as of sorrow to those of her sister kingdom. No event in English history has produced a greater number of poetical effusions than the field of Floddon.

In 1664 was published "A metrical History of the battle of Floddon," the composition, as it is conjectured, of some North-country schoolmaster in the time of Q. Elizabeth. Two different editions of this old piece appeared in the year 1774. One in a small 12mo. with the name of J. Benson Philomath. The other was printed at Berwick, from an old MS. and attended with a number of annotations and historical remarks, with other interesting, useful, and curious communications, by the reverend Mr. Lambe, vicar of Norham upon Tweed. It was likewise printed, though very incorrectly, by old Gent of York. And there is a MS. copy of it in the British Museum (Harl. Lib. 3526).

In the above library are also the following poems relative to this event.

No. 367. beginning—

"Now lette us talke of the mounte of Floden."

No. 293. "A Ballate of the Batalle of Flodene-feeld,".... (in praise of the Stanleys, and the men of Lancashire and Cheshire).

No. 2252. beginning—

"As I lay musing myself alone."

And in the same number is that beginning—

"O Rex Regum in thy Realme celestial,"

printed in "The Mirror for Magistrates," which, with another by Ulpian Fulwell, is inserted by Mr. Lambe in his Appendix, No. VI. and VIII. p. 133. 153.

Skelton, in his rude way, exults very much on the subject. See his *Works*, ed. 1736, p. 102. Lambes *Appendix*, No. VII. p. 143.

A defeat is never a favourite and rarely a successful topic of poetry. The Scotish muse must however on this occasion be allowed the bays. The beautiful and affecting little ballad which appears to have been composed immediately after the battle, beginning—

"I've heard of a lilting,"

is as sweet and natural a piece of elegiac poetry as any language can boast.

A MS. poem on the battle of Flowden hill is mentioned in the catalogue of the Advocates Library at Edinburgh; but appeared, on enquiry, to be either lost or mislaid.

The following ballad may possibly be as ancient as any thing we have on the subject. It is given from " The most pleasant and delectable history of John Winchcomb, otherwise called Jack of Newberry," written by Thomas Deloney, who thus speaks of it:

" In disgrace of the Scots, and in remembrance of the famous atchieved victory, the commons of England made this song: which TO THIS DAY is not forgotten of many."

It will not be contended, however, that the ballad here printed exhibits the genuine English of Henry the 8ths time. Honest Thomas, no doubt, like greater editors, had too refined a taste to prefer accuracy and fidelity to pleasing the eyes or tickling the ears of his readers.

This author is mentioned by Kempe, (*Nine Days Wonder*, 1600, 4to.) as "the great ballade maker T. D. or Thomas Deloney, chronicler of the memorable Lives of the Six Yeomen of the West, JACK OF NEWBERY, The Gentle Craft, and such like honest men, omitted by Stowe, Hollinshed, Grafton, Hall, Froissart, and the rest of those well-deserving writers." (Warton, *Hist. Eng. Poet.* iii. 430.) He had satirized Kempe in what he calls "abhominable ballets." Nashe, in his " Have with you to Saffronwalden, or, Gabriell Harveys Hunt is up," 1596, 4to. calls him " Thomas Deloney the balleting silke-weaver," and says that he "hath rime inough for all myracles, and wit to make a *Garland of good will* more than the premisses, with an Epistle of *Momus* and *Zoylus:* whereas his Muse from the first peeping foorth, hath stood at livery at an Ale-house wishe, never exceeding a penny a quart day nor night; and this deare yeare, together with the silencing of his looms, scarce that; he being constrained to betake him to carded Ale: whence it proceedeth, that since *Candlemas* or his Jigge of *John for the King*, not one merrie dittie will come from him, but *The Thunderbolt against Swearers, Repent England repent*, and *The Strange Judgements of God*."

" John Winscombe, called commonly Jack of Newberry," as we are told by Fuller, " was the most considerable clothier (without fancy and fiction) England ever beheld... In the expedition to Flodden-field, he marched with an hundred of his own men, (as well armed, and better clothed ' than' any) to shew that the painfull to use their hands in peace, could be valiant, and imploy their armes in war. He feasted King Henry the eighth and his first Queen Katherine at his own house, extant at Newberry at this day."

Worthies in Bark-shire. Warton says, that *Jack of Newbury* was entered in the Stationers book to T. Myllington, Mar. 7, 1596; and the *Gentle Craft* to Ralph Blore, Oct. 19, 1597. Deloney narrowly escaped being committed to the Counter, by the Lord Mayor, in 1596, for ridiculing the Queen, and book of orders, about the dearth of corn, in a "scurrilous ballad." See Stows *" Survey"* by Strype, 1720, b. 5. p. 333.

KING Jamie hath made a vow,
    Keep it well if he may,
That he will be at lovely London,
    Upon saint James his day.

" Upon saint James his day, at noon,
    At fair London will I be ;
And all the lords in merry Scotland,
    They shall dine there with me."

Then bespake good queen Margaret,
    The tears fell from her eye,   10
Leave off these wars most noble king,
    Keep your fidelity.

The water runs swift, and wonderous deep,
    From bottom unto the brim ;
My brother Henry hath men good enough,
    England is hard to win.

Away, (quoth he,) with this silly fool,
    In prison fast let her lye ;
For she is come of the English blood,
    And for these words she shall die.   20

That day made many a fatherless child,
   And many a widow poor;
And many a Scottish gay lady
   Sate 'weeping' in her bower.

With that bespake lord Thomas Howard,
   The queens chamberlain, that day,
If that you put queen Margaret to death,
   Scotland shall rue it alway.

Then, in a rage, king Jamie did say,
   Away with this foolish mome!   30
He shall be hang'd, and the other burn'd,
   So soon as I come home.

At Flodden-field the Scots came in,
   Which made our English-men fain;
At Bramstone-green this battel was seen,
   There was king Jamie slain.

Then, presently, the Scots did fly,
   Their cannons they left behind;
Their ensigns gay were won all away,
   Our souldiers did beat them blind.   40

To tell you plain, twelve thousand were slain,
   That to the fight did stand;
And many a prisoner took that day,
   The best in all Scotland.

          V. 24. sweeping.

Jack, with a fether, was lapt all in lether,
  His boastings were all in vain;
He had such a chance, with new morrice-dance,
  He never went home again.

XX.

THE UNGRATEFUL KNIGHT

AND

FAIR FLOWER OF NORTHUMBERLAND,

BY THE SAME,

—— is preserved in the *History of Jack of Newbery*, already mentioned, where it is thus introduced. " His Majesty [i. e. K. Henry the 8th, who was then upon a visit to Jack] came next among the spinners and carders, who were merrily a working: .... The King and Queen and all the nobility heedfully beheld these women, who for the most part were very fair and comely creatures; and were all attired alike from top to toe. Then (after due reverence) the maidens in dulcet manner chanted out this song, two of them singing the ditty, and all the rest bearing the burden."

It was a knight, in Scotland born,
  (Follow, my love, come over the strand),
Was taken prisoner and left forlorn,
  Even by the good earl of Northumberland.

Then was he cast in prison strong,
  (Follow, my love, ' come ' over the strand),
Where he could not walk nor lye along,
  Even by the good earl of Northumberland.

[V. 6. leap.]

And as in sorrow thus he lay,
   (Follow, my love, come over the strand),   10
The earl[s] sweet daughter walks that way,
   And she is the fair flower of Northumberland.

And passing by, like an angel bright,
   (Follow, my love, come over the strand),
The prisoner had of her a sight,
   And she the fair flower of Northumberland.

And aloud to her this knight did cry
   (Follow, my love, come over the strand),
The salt tears standing in his eye,
   And she the fair flower of Northumberland.   20

Fair lady, he said, take pity on me
   (Follow, my love, come over the strand),
And let me not in prison die,
   And you the fair flower of Northumberland.

" Fair sir, how should I take pity on thee
   (Follow, my love, come over the strand),
Thou being a foe to our country,
   And I the fair flower of Northumberland."

Fair lady, I am no foe, he said,
   (Follow, my love, come over the strand),   30
Through thy sweet love here was I stay'd,
   For thee, the fair flower of Northumberland.

" Why should'st thou come here for love of me
   (Follow, my love, come over the strand),
Having wife and children in thy country,
   And I the fair flower of Northumberland?"

" I swear, by the blessed trinity
   (Follow, my love, come over the strand),
I have no wife nor children I,
   Nor dwelling at home in merry Scotlànd.   40

If, courteously, you will set me free
   (Follow, my love, come over the strand),
I vow that I will marry thee,
   So soon as I come in fair Scotlànd.

Thou shalt be a lady of castles and towers
   (Follow, my love, come over the strand),
And sit, like a queen, in princely bowers,
   When I am at home in fair Scotlànd."

Then parted hence this lady gay
   (Follow, my love, come over the strand),   50
And got her fathers ring away,
   To help this knight into fair Scotlànd.

Likewise, much gold she got by sleight
   (Follow, my love, come over the strand),
And all to help this forlorn knight,
   To wend from her father to fair Scotlànd.

Two gallant steeds, both good and able
   (Follow, my love, come over the strand),
She, likewise, took out of the stable,
   To ride with the knight into fair Scotlànd.   60

And to the jaylor she sent this ring
   (Follow, my love, come over the strand),
The knight from prison forth 'to' bring,
   To wend with her into fair Scotlànd.

This token set the prisoner free
   (Follow, my love, come over the strand),
Who straight went to this fair lady,
   To wend with her into fair Scotlànd.

A gallant steed he did bestride
   (Follow, my love, come over the strand),   70
And, with the lady, away did ride,
   And she the fair flower of Northumberlànd.

They rode till they came to a water clear
   (Follow, my love, come over the strand):
" Good sir, how should I follow you here,
   And I the fair flower of Northumberland?

The water is rough and wonderful deep
   (Follow, my love, come over the strand),
And on my saddle I shall not keep,
   And I the fair flower of Northumberlànd."   80

Fear not the foard, fair lady, quoth he
   (Follow, my love, come over the strand),
For long I cannot stay for thee,
   And thou the fair flower of Northumberlànd.

The lady prickt her wanton steed
   (Follow, my love, come over the strand),
And over the river swom with speed,
   And she the fair flower of Northumberlànd.

From top to toe all wet was she
   (Follow, my love, come over the strand):   90
" This have I done, for love of thee,
   And I the fair flower of Northumberlànd."

Thus rode she all one winters night
   (Follow, my love, come over the strand),
Till Edenborough they saw in sight,
   The fairest town in all Scotlànd.

Now chuse, quoth he, thou wanton flower
   (Follow, my love, come over the strand),
‘ Whether ’ thou wilt be my paramour,
   Or get thee home to Northumberlànd.   100

For I have wife and children five
   (Follow, my love, come over the strand),
In Edenborough they be alive,
   Then get thee home to fair Englànd.

This favour thou shalt have to boot
   (Follow, my love, come over the strand),
I 'le have ‘ thy ’ horse, go thou on foot,
   Go, get thee home, to Northumberlànd.—

O false and faithless knight! quoth she
   (Follow, my love, come over the strand),   110
And can'st thou deal so bad with me,
   And I the fair flower of Northumberlànd?

Dishonour not a ladies name
   (Follow, my love, come over the strand),
But draw thy sword and end my shame,
   And I the fair flower of Northumberlànd.

He took her from her stately steed
   (Follow, my love, come over the strand),
And left her there, in extream need,
   And she the fair flower of Northumberlànd.   120

Then sat she down full heavily
   (Follow, my love, come over the strand);
At length two knights came riding by,
   Two gallant knights of fair Englànd.

She fell down humbly, on her knee
   (Follow, my love, come over the strand),
Saying, Courteous 'knights' take pity on me,
   And I the fair flower of Northumberlànd.

I have offended my father dear
   (Follow, my love, come over the strand),   130
And by a false knight that brought me here,
   From the good earl of Northumberlànd.

They took her up behind them then
   (Follow, my love, come over the strand),
And brought her to her father again,
   And he the good earl of Northumberlànd.

All you fair maidens be warned by me
   (Follow, my love, come over the strand),
Scots never were true, nor never will be,
   To lord, nor lady, nor fair Englànd.   140

XXI.

THE HEIR OF LINNE.

This old and excellent ballad was first given from a copy in dr. Percys folio manuscript. The judgement of that learned editor, who says, From the Scotish phrases here and there discernable in this poem, it should seem to have been, originally, composed beyond the Tweed, it was inserted, by the present editor, in the second volume of "Scotish songs;" but he, being convinced that there is not a single word throughout which is not as much English as Scotish, will cause it to be ejected out of that collection, if it ever arrive at a second edition. As proof, with what licentiousness and corruption the editor of *Reliques of ancient English poetry* had, originally, treated this ballad, appears from his own words: "In the present edition [1794], several ancient readings are restored from the folio MS:" and if one could obtain a sight of that tattered fragment, it is highly probable, that several modern interpolations still remain.

LITHE and listen, gentlemen,
    To sing a song I will begin:
It is of a lord of faire Scotlànd,
    Which was the unthrifty heire of Linne.

His father was a right good lord,
    His mother a lady of high degree;
But they, alas! were dead, him froe,
    And he loved keeping companie.

To spend the daye with merry cheare,
    To drinke and revell every night,   10.
To card and dice from eve to morne,
    It was, I ween, his hearts delighte.

To ride, to runne, to rant, to roare,
    To alwaye spend and never spare,
I wott, an' it were the king himselfe,
    Of gold and fee he mote be bare.

Soe fares the unthrifty lord of Linne,
    Till all his gold is gone and spent;
And he maun sell his landes so broad,
    His house and landes and all his rent.   20

His father had a keen stewàrde,
    And John o' the Scales was called hee:
But John is become a gentel-man,
    And John has gott both gold and fee.

Sayes, Welcome, welcome, lord of Linne,
    Let nought disturb thy merry cheere,
Iff thou wilt sell thy landes soe broad,
    Good store of gold I 'le give thee heere.

" My gold is gone, my money is spent;
    My lande nowe take it unto thee: 30
Give me the golde, good John o' the Scales,
    And thine for aye the lande shall bee."

Then John he did him to record draw,
    And John he gave him a gods-pennie;
But for every pounde that John agreed,
    The land, I wis, was well worth three.

He told the gold upon the board,
    He was right glad his land to winne:
" The gold is thine, the land is mine,
    And now I 'le be the lord of Linne."   40

Thus he hath sold his land soe broad,
   Both hill and holt, and moore and fenne,
All but a poore and lonesome lodge,
   That stood far off in a lonely glenne.

For soe he to his father hight:
   My sonne, whenne I am gonne, say'd he,
Then thou wilt spend thy lande so broad,
   And thou wilt spend thy gold so free:

But sweare me nowe upon the roode,
   That lonesome lodge thou 'lt never spend;   50
For when all the world doth frown on thee,
   Thou there shalt find a faithful friend.

The heire of Linne is full of golde:
   And come with me, my friends, sayd hee,
Let 's drinke and rant and merry make
   And he that spares, ne'er mote he thee.

They ranted, drank and merry made,
   Till all his gold it waxed thinne;
And then his friendes they slunk away;
   They left the unthrifty heire of Linne.   60

He had never a penny left in his purse,
   Never a penny left but three,
And one was brass and another was lead
   And another it was white money.

Nowe well-aday, sayd the heire of Linne,
   Nowe well-aday and woe is mee,
For when I was the lord of Linne,
   I never wanted gold nor fee.

But many a trustye friend have I,
   And why shold I feel dole or care?
I 'le borrow of them all by turnes,
   So need I not be never bare.

But one, I wis, was not at home,
   Another had payd his gold away;
Another call'd him thriftless loone,
   And bade him, sharpely, wend his way.

Now well-a-day, sayd the heire of Linne,
   Now well-a-day and woe is me!
For when I had my landes so broad,
   On me they lived right merrilee.

To beg my bread from door to door,
   I wis, it were a brenning shame:
To rob and steal it were a sinne:
   To worke my limbs I cannot frame.

Now I 'le away to [the] lonesome lodge,
   For there my father bade me wend:
When all the world should frown on mee,
   I there shold find a trusty friend.

Away then hyed the heire of Linne,
   O'er hill and holt and moor and fenne,
Until he came to [the] lonesome lodge,
   That stood so lowe in a lonely glenne.

He looked up, he looked downe,
   In hope some comfort for to winne,
But bare and lothly were the walles:
   Here's sorry cheare, quo' the heire of Linne.

The little windowe dim and darke
   Was hung with ivy, brere and yewe;
No shimmering sunn here ever shone;
   No halesome breeze here ever blew.   100

No chair, ne table he mote spye,
   No chearful hearth, ne welcome bed,
Nought save a rope with renning noose,
   That dangling hung up o'er his head:

And over it in broad lettèrs,
   These words were written so plain to see:
Ah! graceless wretch, hast spent thine all,
   And brought thyselfe to penurie?

All this my bodeing mind misgave,
   I therefor left this trusty friend: 110
Let it now sheeld thy foule disgrace,
   And all thy shame and sorrows end.

Sorely shent wi' this rebuke,
   Sorely shent was the heire of Linne,
His heart, I wis, was near to-brast,
   With guilt and sorrowe, shame and sinne.

Never a word spake the heire of Linne,
   Never a word he spake but three:
This is a trusty friend indeed,
   And is right welcome unto mee.   120

Then round his necke the corde he drewe,
   And sprang aloft with his bodie:
When lo! the ceiling burst in twaine,
   And to the ground came tumbling hee.

Astonyed lay the heire of Linne,
  Ne knew if he were live or dead,
At length he loked and sawe a bille,
  And in it a key of gold so redd.

He took the bill and lookt it on,
  Strait good comfort found he there :   130
It told him of a hole in the wall,
  In which there stood three chests in-fere.

Two were full of the beaten golde,
  The third was full of white monèy;
And over them in broad lettèrs
  These words were written so plaine to see :

Once more, my sonne, I sette thee cleare,
  Amend thy life and follies past;
For, but thou amend thee of thy life,
  That rope must be thy end at last :   140

And let it bee, sayd the heire of Linne,
  And let it bee, but if I amend :
For here I will make mine avow,
  This reade shall guide me to the end.

Away then went, with a merry cheare,
  Away then went the heire of Linne,
I wis, he neither ceased ne blanne,
  Till John o' the Scales house he did winne :

And when he came to John'o' the Scales,
  Up at the speere then looked hee;   150
There sate three lords upon a rowe,
  Were drinking of the wine so free :

And John himself sate at the bord-head,
    Because now lord of Linne was hee,
I pray thee, he sayd, good John o' the Scales,
    One forty pence for to lend mee.

Away, away, thou thriftless loone;
    Away, away, this may not bee:
For Christs curse on my head, he sayd,
    If ever I trust thee one pennie.   160

Then bespake the heire of Linne,
    To John o' the Scales wife then spake hee:
Madame, some almes on me bestowe,
    I pray for sweet saint Charitie.

" Away, away, thou thriftless loone,
    I swear thou gettest no almes of mee;
For if we shold hang any losel heere,
    The first we wold begin with thee."

Then bespake a good fellòwe,
    Which sat at John o' the Scales his bord: 170
Sayd, Turn againe, thou heire of Linne;
    Some time thou wast a well good lord:

Some time a good fellow thou hast been,
    And sparedst not thy gold and fee,
Therefore I'le lend thee forty pence
    And other forty if need bee:

And ever, I pray thee, John o' the Scales,
    To let him sit in thy companie:
For well I wot thou hadst his land,
    And a good bargain it was to thee.   180

Up then spake him John o' the Scales,
    All wood he answered him againe:
Now Christs curse on my head, he sayd,
    But I did lose by that bargaine:

And here I proffer thee, heire of Linne,
    Before these lords so faire and free,
Thou shalt have it backe again better cheape,
    By a hundred markes, than I had it of thee.

I drawe you to record, lords, he said.
    With that he cast him a gods-pennie: 190
Now by my fay, sayd the heire of Linne,
    And here, good John, is thy money:

And he pull'd forth three bagges of gold
    And layd them down upon the bord:
All woe-begone was John o' the Scales,
    Soe shent he cold say never a word.

He told him forth the good red gold,
    He told it forth [with] mickle dinne:
" The gold is thine, the land is mine
    And now I'me againe the lord of Linne."   200

Sayes, Have thou here, thou good fellòw!
    Forty pence thou didst lend mee:
Now I am againe the lord of Linne,
    And forty pounds I will give thee.

Ile make 'thee' keeper of my forrèst,
    Both of the wild deere and the tame;
For, but I reward thy bounteous heart,
    I wis, good fellow, I were to blame.

Now well-a-day! sayth Joan o' the Scales:
   Now well-a-day! and woe is my life!   210
Yesterday I was lady of Linne,
   Now I'm but John o' the Scales his wife.

Now fare thee well, sayd the heire of Linne,
   Farewell now, John o' the Scales, said hee:
Christs curse light on me if ever again
   I bring my lands in jeopardỳ.

XXII.

LORD THOMAS AND FAIR ELEANOR.

LORD Thomas he was a bold forestèr,
   And a chaser of the kings deer;
Fair Eleanor was a fine womàn,
   And Lord Thomas he lov'd her dear.

Come riddle my riddle, dear mother, he said,
   And riddle us both as one;
Whether I shall marry with fair Eleanòr,
   And let the brown girl alone?

The brown girl she has got houses and lands,
   Fair Eleanor she has got none,   10
Therefor I charge thee, on my blessìng,
   To bring me the brown girl home.

And as it befell on a high holidày,
   As many did more beside,
Lord Thomas he went to fair Eleanòr,
   That should have been his bride.

But when he came to fair Eleanors bower,
    He knocked there at the ring,
But who was so ready as fair Eleanòr,
    To let lord Thomas within.   20

What news, what news, lord Thomas? she said,
    What news hast thou brought unto me?
I am come to bid thee to my wedding,
    And that is bad news for thee.

O god forbid, lord Thomas, she said,
    That such a thing should be done;
I thought to have been thy bride my own self,
    And you to have been the bridegroom.

Come riddle my riddle, dear mother, she said,
    And riddle it all in one;   30
Whether I shall go to lord Thomases wedding,
    Or whether I shall tarry at home?

There's many that are your friends, daughtèr,
    And many that are your foe,
Therefor I charge you, on my blessing,
    To lord Thomases wedding don't go.

There's many that are my friends, mother,
    If a thousand more were my foe,
Betide my life, or betide my death,
    To lord Thomases wedding I'll go.   40

She clothed herself in gallant attire,
    And her merry men all in green,
And as they rid through every town,
    They took her to have been a queen.

But when she came to lord Thomases gate,
    She knocked there at the ring;
But who was so ready as lord Thomàs,
    To let fair Eleanor in.

Is this your bride? fair Ellen she said,
    Methinks she looks wonderous brown;   50
You might have had as fair a womàn
    As ever trod on the ground.

Despise her not, fair Ellen, he said,
    Despise her not unto me;
For better I love thy little-fingèr,
    Than all her whole bodỳ.

This brown bride had a little penknife,
    That was both long and sharp,
And betwixt the short ribs and the long,
    She prick'd fair Eleanòr to the heart.   60

Oh! Christ now save thee, lord Thomas, he said,
    Methinks thou look'st wonderous 'wan;'
Thou wast us'd for to look with as fresh a colòur,
    As ever the sun shin'd on.

Oh! art thou blind, lord Thomas? she said,
    Or can'st thou not very well see?
Oh! dost thou not see my own hearts blood
    Runs trickling down my knee?

Lord Thomas he had a sword by his side;
    As he walk'd about the hall,   70
He cut off his brides head from her shouldèrs;
    And he threw it against the wall.

    [*V.* 62. wain.]

He set the hilt against the ground,
   And the point against his heart;
There was never three lovers that ever met
   More sooner 'that' did depart.

XXIII.

FAIR MARGARET AND SWEET WILLIAM.

As it fell out upon a day,
   Two lovers they sat on a hill;
They sat together a long summers day,
   And could not talk their fill.

I see no harm by you, Margarèt,
   And you see none by me;
Before to-morrow at eight o'clock
   A rich wedding you shall see.

Fair Margaret sat in her bower-window,
   A combing of her hair;   10
There she espied sweet William and his bride,
   As they were a riding near.

Down she laid her ivory comb,
   And up she bound her hair;
She went away 'fast' from the bower,
   But never more came there.

       [*V*. 76. they.]
       [*V*. 15. first.]

When day was gone, and night was come,
    And all men fast asleep,
Then came the spirit of fair Margarèt,
    And stood at Williams bed feet*.   20

" God give you joy, you true lovèrs,
    In bride-bed fast asleep;
Lo! I am going to my grass-green grave,
    And I am in my winding sheet."

When day was come, and night was gone,
    And all men wak'd from sleep,
Sweet William to his lady said,
    My dear, I've cause to weep.

I dream'd a dream, my dear lad̀y,
    Such dreams are never good;   30
I dream'd my bower was full of red ' wine,'
    And my bride-bed full of blood.

" Such dreams, such dreams, my honour'd sir,
    They never do prove good;
To dream thy bower was full of ' wine '
    And thy bride-bed full of blood."

He called [up] his merry men all,
    By one, by two, and by three,
Saying, I'll away to fair Margarets bower,
    By the leave of my lad̀y.   40

* To this stanza [as introduced by Fletcher in " The Knight of the burning pestle "] the public is indebted for the beautiful and pathetic ballad of *Margarets ghost*, by Mallet.

[*V.* 31. 35. swine.]

And when he came to fair Margarets bower,
   He knocked at the ring;
So ready were her seven brethrèn,
   To let sweet William in.

Then he turn'd up the covering-sheet:
   " Pray let me see the dead;
Methinks she looks both pale and wan,
   She has lost her cherry red.

I'll do more for thee, Margarèt,
   Than any of thy kin;
For I will kiss thy pale wan lips,
   Though a smile I cannot win."

With that bespoke the seven brethrèn,
   Making most piteous moan,
You may go kiss your jolly brown dame,
   And let our sister alone.

" If I do kiss my jolly brown dame,
   I do but what is right;
For I made no vow to your sister dear,
   By day, nor yet by night.

Pray tell me, then, how much you'll deal,
   Of white bread and 'of' wine:
So much as is dealt at her funeral to day,
   To-morrow shall be dealt at mine."

Fair Margaret died to-day, to-day,
   Sweet William he died the morrow;
Fair Margaret died for pure true love,
   Sweet William he died for sorrow.

       [*V*. 62. your.]

Margaret was buried in the lower chancel,
    And William in the higher;   70
Out of her breast there sprang a rose,
    And out of his a briar.

They grew as high as the church-top,
    Till they could grow no higher;
And there they grew in a true lovers knot,
    Which made all the people admire.

Then came the clerk of the parish,
    As you 'the' truth shall hear,
And by misfortune cut them down,
    Or they had now been there.   80

XXIV.

BATEMANS TRAGEDY.

The full title of the old copy is, "A Godly Warning for all Maidens, by the Example of Gods Judegment shewed upon one Jermans Wife of Clifton, in the County of Nottingham, who, lying in child-bed, was born away, and never heard of after." A tragedy entitled *The Vow breaker*, written by one William Sampson, and printed in 1636, is founded on this ballad, and quotes two or three verses from it, as "a lamentable new ditty."

You dainty dames, so finely fram'd
    Of beautys chiefest mold,
And you that trip it up and down,
    Like lambs in Cupids fold,

[*V.* 77. the.]

Here is a lesson to be learn'd;
   A lesson, in my mind,
For such as will prove false in love,
   And bear a faithless mind.

Not far from Nottingham, of late,
   In Clifton, as I hear,   10
There dwelt a fair and comely dame,
   For beauty without peer;
Her cheeks were like the crimson-rose;
   Yet, as you may perceive,
The fairest face, the falsest heart,
   And soonest will deceive.

This gallant dame she was belov'd
   Of many in that place;
And many sought, in marriage-bed,
   Her body to embrace: 20
At last a proper handsome youth,
   Young Bateman call'd by name,
In hopes to make a married wife,
   Unto this maiden came.

Such love and liking there was found,
   That he, from all the rest,
Had stol'n away the maidens heart,
   And she did love him best:
Then plighted promise secretly
   Did pass between them two,   30
That nothing could, but death itself,
   This true loves knot undo.

He brake a piece of gold in twain,
    One half to her he gave;
The other, as a pledge, quoth he,
    Dear heart, myself will have.
If I do break my vow, quoth she,
    While I remain alive,
May never thing I take in hand
    Be seen at all to thrive.   40

This passed on for two months space,
    And then this maid began
To settle love and liking too
    Upon another man:
One Jerman who a widower was,
    Her husband needs must be,
Because he was of greater wealth,
    And better in degree.

Her vows and promise lately made
    To Bateman she denied;   50
And in despite of him and his
    She utterly defied.
Well then, quoth he, if it be so,
    That you will me forsake,
And, like a false and forsworn wretch,
    Another husband take.

Thou shalt not live one quiet hour,
    For surely I will have
Thee, either now alive, or dead,
    When I am laid in grave: 60

Thy faithless mind thou shalt repent;
    Therefor be well assur'd,
When, for thy sake, thou hear'st report
    What torments I endur'd.

But mark how Bateman died for love,
    And finish'd up his life,
That very day she married was,
    And made old Jermans wife;
For with a strangling-cord, god wot,
    Great moan was made therefor,
He hang'd himself in desperate sort,
    Before the brides own door.

Whereat such sorrow pierc'd her heart,
    And troubled sore her mind,
That she could never, after that,
    One day of comfort find;
And wheresoever she did go,
    Her fancy did surmise,
Young Batemans pale and ghastly ghost
    Appear'd before her eyes.

When she in bed at night did lie,
    Betwixt her husbands arms,
In hope thereby to sleep and rest
    In safety without harms;
Great cries and grievous groans she heard,
    A voice that sometimes 'cried'
O thou art she that I must have,
    And will not be denied.

        [*V.* 86. said.]

But she [then] being big with child,
    Was, for the infants sake,   90
Preserved from the spirits power,
    No vengeance could it take:
The babe unborn did safely keep,
    As god appointed so,
His mothers body from the fiend
    That sought her overthrow.

But being of her burden eas'd,
    And safely brought to bed,
Her care and grief began anew
    And farther sorrow bred: 100
And of her friends she did intreat,
    Desiring them to stay;
Out of the bed, quoth she, this night,
    I shall be born away.

Here comes the spirit of my love,
    With pale and ghastly face,
Who till he bear me hence away,
    Will not depart this place;
Alive or dead I'm his by right,
    And he will surely have,   110
In spite of me and all the world,
    What I by promise gave.

O watch with me this night, I pray;
    And see you do not sleep:
No longer than you be awake
    My body can you keep.

All promised to do their best;
   Yet nothing could suffice
In middle of the night to keep
   Sad slumber from their eyes.

So being all full fast asleep,
   To them unknown which way,
The child-bed-woman that woeful night,
   From thence was born away;
And to what place no creature knew,
   Nor to this day can tell:
As strange a thing as ever yet
   In any age befell.

You maidens that desire to love,
   And would good husbands choose,
To him that you do vow to love,
   By no means do refuse:
For god, that hears all secret oaths,
   Will dreadful vengeance take
On such that of a wilful vow
   Do slender reckoning make.

XXV.

THE WANDERING PRINCE OF TROY.

The old printed copies, being palpably corrupt, have been judiciously corrected by the ingenious dr. Percy, whose emendations are here adopted, though not without proper marks of distinction.

WHEN Troy town, [had] for ten years 'past'
    Withstood the Greeks, in manful wise,
Then did their foes encrease so fast,
    That to resist 'nought' could suffice:
Waste lie those walls that were so good,
And corn now grows where Troy town stood.

Æneas, wandering prince of Troy,
    When he for land long time had sought,
At length, 'arriving' with great joy,
    To mighty Carthage walls was brought;   10
Where Dido queen, with sumptuous feast,
Did entertain this wandering guest.

And, as in hall at meat they sate,
    The queen, desirous news to hear,
'Says, of thy Troys unhappy fate'
    Declare to me thou Trojan dear:
The heavy hap, and chance so bad,
Which thou, poor wandering prince, hast had.

And then, anon, this comely knight,
    With words demure, as he could well,   20

Of 'their' unhappy ten years 'fight'
   So true a tale began to tell,
With words so sweet, and sighs so deep,
That oft he made them all to weep.

And then a thousand sighs he 'fet,'
   And every sigh brought tears amain;
That where he sate the place was wet,
   As he had seen those wars again:
So that the queen, with ruth therefore,
Said, worthy prince, enough, no more.   30

The darksome night apace grew on,
   And twinkling stars in skies were spread,
And he his doleful tale had 'done,'
   And every one was laid in bed;
Where they full sweetly took their rest,
Save only Didos boiling breast.

This silly woman never slept,
   But in her chamber, all alone,
As one unhappy, always wept,
   And to the walls she made her moan;   40
That she should still desire in vain
The thing that she could not obtain.

And thus in grief she spent the night,
   Till twinkling stars from sky were fled,
And Phœbus, with his glittering 'light,'
   Through misty clouds appeared red;
Then tidings came to her anon,
That all the Trojan ships were gone.

And then the queen, with bloody knife,
   Did arm her heart as hard as stone,   50
Yet, somewhat loth to lose her life,
   In woeful wise she made her moan;
And, rolling on her careful bed,
With sighs and sobs, these words she said:

O wretched Dido queen, quoth she,
   I see thy end approaching near;
For he is gone away from thee,
   Whom thou did'st love, and 'hold' so dear:
Is he then gone, and passed by?
O heart, prepare thyself to die.   60

Though Reason would thou should'st forbear,
   And stay thy hand from bloody stroke;
Yet Fancy says thou should'st not fear,
   Who fettereth thee in Cupids yoke.
Come Death, quoth she, resolve my smart:—
And, with these words, she pierc'd her heart.

When Death had pierc'd the tender heart,
   Of Dido, Carthaginian queen,
And bloody knife did end the smart,
   Which she sustain'd in woeful teen,—   70
Æneas being shipp'd and gone,
Whose flattery caused all her moan.—

Her funeral most costly made,
   And all things furnish'd mournfully;
Her body fine in mold was laid,
   Where it consumed speedily:

Her sisters tears her tomb bestrew'd;
Her subjects grief their kindness shew'd.

Then was Æneas in an isle,
   In Grecia, where he liv'd long space,   80
Whereas her sister, in short while,
   Writ to him to his vile disgrace;
In phrase of letters to her mind,
She told him plain he was unkind.

False-hearted wretch, quoth she, thou art;
   And treacherously thou hast betray'd
Unto thy lure a gentle heart,
   Which unto thee such welcome made;
My sister dear, and Carthage joy,
Whose folly wrought her dire annoy.   90

Yet, on her death-bed when she lay,
   She pray'd for thy prosperity,
Beseeching heaven, that every day
   Might breed thy great felicity:
Thus, by thy means, I lost a friend;
Heaven send thee such untimely end!

When he these lines, full fraught with gall,
   Perused had, and weigh'd them right,
His lofty courage then did fall,
   And straight appeared in his sight   100
Queen Didos ghost, both grim and pale;
Which made this gallant soldier quail.

Æneas, quoth this grisly ghost,
   My whole delight while I did live,
Thee of all men I loved most;
   My fancy and my will did give:
For entertainment I thee gave,
Unthankfully thou 'dug'st' my grave.

Therefore, prepare thy fleeting soul
   To wander with me in the air;   110
Where deadly grief shall make it howl,
   Because of me thou took'st no care:
Delay no time, thy glass is run,
Thy day is pass'd, thy death is come.

" O stay a while, thou lovely sprite;
   Be not so hasty to convey
My soul into eternal night,
   Where it shall ne'er behold bright day.
O do not frown,—thy angry look
Hath ' all my soul with horror shook.'   120

But, woe to me! it is in vain,
   And bootless is my dismal cry;
Time will not be recall'd again,
   Nor thou surcease before I die.
O let me live, to make amends
Unto some of thy dearest friends.

But, seeing thou obdurate art,
   And wilt no pity to me show,
Because from thee I did depart,
   And left unpaid what I did owe,   130

    [*V.* 120. Hath *made my breath my life forsook.*]

> I must content myself to take
> What lot thou wilt with me partake."

And, like one being in a trance,
   A multitude of ugly fiends
About this woeful prince did dance,
   No help he had of any friends;
His body then they took away,
And no man knew his dying day.

XXVI.

THE SPANISH LADYS LOVE.

BY THOMAS DELONEY.

It is printed in "The garland of good will," a collection of songs and ballads which he published before 1596.

WILL you hear a Spanish lady,
   How she woo'd an English man?
Garments gay as rich as may be,
   Deck'd with jewels, had she on:
Of a comely countenance and grace was she,
Both by birth and parentage of high degree.

As his prisoner there he kept her,
   In his hands her life did lie;
Cupids bands did tie them faster,
   By the liking of an eye.   10
In his courteous company was all her joy,
To favour him in any thing she was not coy.

But at last there came commandment
    For to set all ladies free,
With their jewels still adorned,
    None to do them injury.
O, then said this lady gay, full woe is me!
O let me still sustain this kind captivity!

    Gallant captain, show some pity
        To a lady in distress;   20
    Leave me not within this city,
        For to die in heaviness:
Thou hast set, this present day, my body free,
But my heart in prison still remains with thee.

    " How should'st thou, fair lady, love me,
        Whom thou know'st thy countrys foe?
    Thy fair words make me suspect thee;
        Serpents lie where flowers grow."
" All the harm I wish on thee, most courteous knight,
God grant upon my head the same may fully light. 30

    Blessed be the time and season,
        That thou came on Spanish ground;
    If you may our foes be termed,
        Gentle foes we have you found:
With our city, you have won our hearts each one,
Then to your country bear away that is your own."

    " Rest you still, most gallant lady;
        Rest you still and weep no more;
    Of fair flowers you have plenty,
        Spain doth yield you wonderous store."—   40

"Spaniards fraught with jealousy we oft do find,
But Englishmen throughout the world are counted
   kind.

Leave me not unto a Spaniard,
   Thou alone enjoy'st my heart;
I am lovely, young, and tender,
   Love is likewise my desert:
Still to serve thee day and night my mind is prest;
The wife of every Englishman is counted bless'd."

"It would be a shame, fair lady,
   For to bear a woman hence;   50
English soldiers never carry
   Any such without offence."
"I will quickly change myself, if it be so,
And like a page will follow thee, where'er thou go."

"I have neither gold nor silver
   To maintain thee in this case,
And to travel is great charges,
   As you know, in every place."
"My chains and jewels every one shall be thy own,
And eke ten thousand pounds in gold that lies
   unknown."   60

"On the seas are many dangers,
   Many storms do there arise,
Which will be to ladies dreadful,
   And force tears from watery eyes."
"Well in troth I shall endure extremity,
For I could find in heart to lose my life for thee.'

" Courteous lady, leave this ' fancy,'
  Here comes all that breeds the strife;
I, in England, have already
  A sweet woman to my wife;   70
I will not falsify my vow for gold nor gain,
Nor yet for all the fairest dames that live in Spain."

" O how happy is that woman
  That enjoys so true a friend!
Many happy days god send her;
  Of my suit I'll make an end:
On my knees I pardon crave for my offence,
Which love and true affection did first commence.

Commend me to that gallant lady,
  Bear to her this chain of gold,   80
With these bracelets, for a token;
  Grieving that I was so bold:
All my jewels, in like sort, take thou with thee;
For they are fitting for thy wife, but not for me.

I will spend my days in prayër,
  Love and all her laws defy;
In a nunnery I will shroud me,
  Far from any company:
But, ere my prayers have an end, be sure of this,
To pray for thee and for thy love I will not miss.   90

Thus farewell, most gallant captain!
  Farewell ' too ' my hearts content!
Count not Spanish ladies wanton,
  Though to thee my mind was bent!

[*V.* 67. folly.]   [*V.* 92. to.]

Joy and prosperity go still with thee!"
" The like fall 'ever to' thy share, most fair lady."

XXVII.

THE LADYS FALL.

MARK well my heavy doleful tale,
    You loyal lovers all,
And heedfully bear in your breast
    A gallant ladys fall.
Long was she woo'd, ere she was won
    To taste a wedded life,
But folly wrought her overthrow,
    Before she was a wife.

Too soon, alas! she gave consent
    To yield unto his will,   10
Though he protested to be true,
    And faithful to her still.
She felt her body alter'd quite,
    Her bright hue waxed pale,
Her fair red cheeks turn'd colour white,
    Her strength began to fail.

So that, with many a sorrowful sigh,
    This beauteous maiden mild,
With grievous heart, perceiv'd herself
    To have conceiv'd with child.   20

[*V*. 96. unto.]

She kept it from her fathers sight,
   As close as close might be,
And so put on her silken gown,
   None might her swelling see.

Unto her lover, secretly,
   Her grief she did bewray,
And, walking with him hand in hand,
   These words to him did say:
Behold, said she, a maids distress,
   By love reduc'd to woe,   30
Behold I go with child by thee,
   But none thereof doth know.

The little babe springs in my womb,
   To hear the fathers voice,
Let it not be a bastard call'd,
   Sith I made thee my choice:
Come, come, my love, perform thy vow,
   And wed me out of hand;
O leave me not in this extreme,
   In grief always to stand!   40

Think on thy former 'promises,'
   Thy vows and oaths each one;
Remember with what bitter tears
   To me thou mad'st thy moan.
Convey me to some secret place,
   And marry me with speed;
Or with thy rapier end my life,
   Ere further shame proceed.

[*V.* 41. promise made.]

Alas! my dearest love, quoth he,
 My greatest joy on earth,   50
Which way can I convey thee hence,
 Without a sudden death?
Thy friends they be of high degree,
 And I of mean estate;
Full hard it is to get thee forth
 Out of thy fathers gate.

"Oh! do not fear to save my fame,
 For if thou taken be,
Myself will step between 'their' swords,
 And take the harm on me: 60
So shall I scape dishonour quite;
 And if I should be slain,
What could they say, but that true love
 Had wrought a ladys bane?

And fear not any further harm;
 Myself will so devise,
That I will ride away with thee,
 Unseen of mortal eyes:
Disguised like some pretty page,
 I'll meet thee in the dark,   70
And all alone I'll come to thee,
 Hard by my fathers park."

And there, quoth he, I'll meet [with] thee,
 If god so lend me life,
And this day month, without all fail,
 I will make thee my wife.

[*V*. 59. the]

Then, with a sweet and loving kiss,
   They parted presently,
And at their parting brinish tears
   Stood in each others eye.   80

At length the wish'd-for day was come,
   On which this beauteous maid,
With 'longing' eyes, and strange attire,
   For her true lover stay'd:
When any person she espied
   Come riding o'er the plain,
She thought it was her own true love,
   But all her hopes were vain.

Then did she weep, and sore bewail
   Her most unhappy state;   90
Then did she speak these woeful words,
   When succourless she sate:
O false, forsworn, and faithless wretch,
   Disloyal to thy love,
Hast thou forgot thy promise made,
   And wilt thou perjur'd prove?

And hast thou now forsaken me,
   In this my great distress,
To end my days in open shame,
   Which thou might'st well redress?   100
Woe worth the time I did believe
   That flattering tongue of thine!
Would god that I had never seen
   The tears of thy false eyne!

[*V.* 83. lovely.]

And thus, with many a sorrowful sigh,
  Homewards she went again;
No rest came in her watery eyes,
  She felt such bitter pain.
In travail strong she fell that night,
  With many a bitter throe;   110
What woeful pangs she then did feel,
  Doth each good woman know.

She called up her waiting-maid,
  That lay at her beds feet,
Who, musing at her mistress' woe,
  Did straight begin to weep.
Weep not, said she, but shut the door,
  And windows round about,
Let none bewail my wretched state,
  But keep all persons out.   120

" O mistress, call your mother dear,
  Of women you have need,
And of some skilful midwifes help,
  That better you may speed."
" Call not my mother, for thy life,
  Nor ' fetch no' women here,
The midwifes help comes all too late
  My death I do not fear."

With that the babe sprang ' from ' her womb,
  No creature being nigh,   130
And with a sigh, which brake her heart,
  This gallant dame did die.

[*V.* 105. a sorrowful sigh.]   [*V.* 126. call the.]   [*V.* 129. *in.*]

' The lovely ' little infant young,
    The mother being dead,
Resign'd his new received breath
    To him that had him made.

Next morning came her lover true,
    Affrighted at this news,
And he for sorrow slew himself,
    Whom each one did accuse.   140
The mother with the new-born babe,
    Were both laid in one grave:
Their parents overcome with woe,
    No joy ' thenceforth ' could have.

Take heed, you dainty damsels all,
    Of flattering words beware,
And of the honour of your names
    Have you a special care.
Too true, alas! this story is,
    As many [a] one can tell: 150
By others harms learn to be wise,
    And you shall do full well.

[*V.* 133. This living.]   [*V.* 144. of them.]

XXVIII.

LITTLE MUSGRAVE AND LADY BARNARD.

The only genuine copy of this old ballad, known to be extant, is preserved in Drydens " collection of miscellaneous poems." Dr. Percy, indeed, by some mistake, gives it as from an old printed copy in the British museum; observing that " In the Pepys collection, is an imitation of this old song, in a different measure, by a more modern pen, with many alterations, but evidently for the worse " It is very true, and not less so, that the only copies in the Museum (for there are two) are more recent impressions of this identical *imitation*.

As it fell [out] one holyday,
   As many be in the year,
When young men and maids together did go
   Their masses and matins to hear.

Little Musgrave came to the church-door,
   The priest he was at mass;
But he had more mind of two fair women,
   Than he had of our ladys grace.

The one of them was clad in green,
   The other was clad in pall;   10
And then came in my lord Barnards wife,
   The fairest among them all.

She cast an eye on little Musgrave,
   As bright as the summer sun;
O then bethought this little Musgrave,
   The ladys heart I have won.

[*V.* 7. the.]

Quoth she, I have lov'd thee, little Musgrave,
    Full long and many a day.
" So have I loved you, lady fair,
    Yet word I never durst say."   20

" I have a bower at Bucklesford-Bury,
    Full daintily bedight,
If thou wilt wend thither, my little Musgrave,
    Thoust lig in mine arms all night."

Quoth he, I thank ye, lady fair,
    This kindness you show to me;
And whether it be to my weal or woe,
    This night will I lig with thee.

All this was heard by a little tiny page,
    By his ladys coach as he ran: 30
Quoth he, though I am my ladys page,
    Yet I am my lord Barnards man.

My lord Barnàrd shall know of this,
    Although I lose a limb,
And ever whereas the bridges were broke,
    He laid him down to swim.

" Asleep or awake, thou lord Barnard,
    As thou art a man of life,
For little Musgrave is at Bucklesford-Bury,
    A-bed with thine own wedded wife."   40

" If this be true, thou little tiny page,
    This thing thou tell'st to me,
Then all the land in Bucklesford-Bury,
    I freely give to thee:

But if 't be a lye, thou little tiny page,
   This thing thou tell'st to me,
On the highest tree in Bucklesford-Bury,
   Then hanged shalt thou be."

He called up his merry men all:
   " Come saddle me my steed;   50
This night must I to Bucklesford-Bury;
   For I never had greater need."

And some of them whistled, and some of them sung,
   And some these words did say,
And ever when as the lord Barnards horn blew,
   Away, thou little Musgrave, away.

" Methinks I hear the throstle-cock,
   Methinks I hear the jay,
Methinks I hear my lord Barnards horn;
   And I would I were away."   60

" Lie still, lie still, thou little Musgrave,
   And huggle me from the cold;
'Tis nothing but a shepherds boy,
   A-driving his sheep to fold.

Is not thy hawk upon the perch?
   Thy steed eats oats and hay;
And thy fair lady in thine arms;
   And would'st thou be away?"

With that my lord Barnard came to the door,
   And lighted upon a stone;   70
He plucked out three silver keys,
   And opened the doors each one.

He lifted up the coverlet,
   He lifted up the sheet:
" How now, how now, thou little Musgrave,
   Dost find my lady sweet?"

I find her sweet, quoth little Musgrave,
   The more 'tis to my pain;
I would gladly give the three hundred pounds
   That I were on yonder plain.   80

" Arise, arise, thou little Musgrave,
   And put thy clothes on;
It shall never be said in my country,
   That I killed a naked man.

I have two swords in one scabbard,
   Full dear they cost my purse,
And thou shalt have the best of them,
   And I will have the worse."

The first stroke that little Musgrave struck,
   He hurt lord Barnard sore;   90
The next stroke that lord Barnard struck
   Little Musgrave ne'er struck more.

With that bespake the lady fair,
   In bed whereas she lay,
Although th' art dead, thou little Musgrave,
   Yet I for thee will pray:

And wish well to thy soul will I,
   So long as I have life;
So will not I do for thee, Barnard,
   Though I am thy wedded wife.   100

He cut her paps from off her breasts;
  Great pity it was to see;
Some drops of this fair ladys heart-blood
  Ran trickling down her knee.

" Woe worth you, woe worth [you], my merry men all,
  You never were born for my good;
Why did you not offer to stay my hand,
  When you ' saw' me wax so wood?

For I have slain the bravest sir knight,
  That ever rode on a steed;   110
So have I done the fairest lady,
  That ever did womans deed."

A grave, a grave, lord Barnard cried,
  To put these lovers in;
But lay my lady o' th' upper hand,
  For she came o' the better kin.

XXIX.

FAIR ROSAMOND.

BY THOMAS DELONEY*.

When as king Henry rul'd this land,
  The second of that name,
Besides the queen, he dearly lov'd
  A fair and comely dame:

---

* See Percys *Reliques*, &c. (edition 1794) III. 405. It is, likewise, in the *Garland of good will.*

Most peerless was her beauty found,
   Her favour, and her face;
A sweeter creature in this world
   Did never prince embrace.

Her crisped locks like threads of gold
   Appear'd to each mans sight;   10
Her sparkling eyes, like orient pearls,
   Did cast a heavenly light;
The blood within her crystal cheeks
   Did such a colour drive,
As if the lily and the rose
   For mastership did strive.

Yea Rosamond, fair Rosamond,
   Her name was called so,
To whom dame Eleanor, our queen,
   Was known a deadly foe.   20
The king therefore, for her defence
   Against the furious queen,
At Woodstock builded such a bower,
   The like was never seen.

Most curiously that bower was built,
   Of stone and timber strong,
One hundred and fifty doors
   Did to this bower belong;
And they so cunningly contriv'd,
   With turnings round about,   30
That none, but with a clew of thread,
   Could enter in or out.

And, for his love and ladys sake,
    That was so fair and bright,
The keeping of this bower he gave
    Unto a valiant knight.
But Fortune, that doth often frown
    Where she before did smile,
The kings delight, the ladys joy,
    Full soon she did beguile.   40

For why, the kings ungracious son,
    Whom he did high advance,
Against his father raised wars,
    Within the realm of France.
But yet before our comely king
    The English land forsook,
Of Rosamond, his lady fair,
    His farewel thus he took:

" My Rosamond, my only Rose,
    That pleasest best mine eye,   50
The fairest flower in all the world
    To feed my fantasy:
The flower of my affected heart,
    Whose sweetness doth excell:
My royal Rose, a thousand times
    I bid thee now farewell.

For I must leave my fairest flower,
    My sweetest Rose, a space,
And cross the seas to famous France,
    Proud rebels to abase.   60

But yet, my Rose, be sure thou shalt
    My coming shortly see,
And in my heart, when hence I am,
    I'll bear my Rose with me."

When Rosamond, that lady bright,
    Did hear the king say so,
The sorrow of her grieved heart
    Her outward looks did show;
And from her clear and crystal eyes
    Tears gushed out apace,   70
Which, like the silver-pearled dew,
    Ran down her comely face.

Her lips, erst like the coral red,
    Did wax both wan and pale,
And, for the sorrow she conceiv'd,
    Her vital spirits did fail;
And falling down all in a swoon,
    Before king Henrys face,
Full oft he in his princely arms
    Her body did embrace: 80

And twenty times, with watry eyes,
    He kiss'd her tender cheek,
Until he had reviv'd again
    Her senses mild and meek.
Why grieves my Rose, my sweetest Rose?
    The king did often say;
Because, quoth she, to bloody wars
    My lord must pass away.

But since your grace, on foreign coasts,
    Among your foes unkind,   90
Must go to hazard life and limb,
    Why should I stay behind?
Nay, rather, let me, like a page,
    Your sword and target bear,
That on my breast the blows may light,
    That should offend you there.

Or let me, in your royal tent,
    Prepare your bed at night,
And with sweet baths refresh your grace
    At your return from fight.   100
So I your presence may enjoy,
    No toil I will refuse;
But, wanting you, my life is death,
    ' Nay, death I'd rather choose!'

" Content thyself, my dearest love;
    Thy rest at home shall be;
In Englands sweet and pleasant soil;
    For travel fits not thee.
Fair ladies brook not bloody wars;
    Sweet peace their pleasures breed;   110
The nourisher of hearts content,
    Which fancy first did feed.

My Rose shall rest in Woodstock bower,
    With musics sweet delight;
Whilst I, among the piercing pikes,
    Against my foes do fight.

        [104. Which doth true love abuse.]

My Rose in robes of pearl and gold,
   With diamonds richly dight,
Shall dance the galliards of my love,
   While I my foes do smite.   120

And you, sir Thomas, whom I trust
   To be my loves defence,
Be careful of my gallant Rose,
   When I am parted hence."
And, therewithall, he fetch'd a sigh,
   As though his heart would break;
And Rosamond, for very grief,
   Not one plain word could speak.

And at their parting well they might
   In heart be grieved sore,   130
After that day fair Rosamond
   The king did see no more:
For when his grace had pass'd the seas,
   And into France was gone,
Queen Eleanor, with envious heart,
   To Woodstock came anon:

And forth she calls this trusty knight,
   Who kept this curious bower,
Who, with his clew of twined thread,
   Came from this famous flower: 140
And when that they had wounded him,
   The queen this thread did get,
And went where lady Rosamond
   Was like an angel set.

But when the queen, with stedfast eye,
    Beheld her heavenly face,
She was amazed in her mind
    At her exceeding grace.
Cast off from thee these robes, she said,
    That rich and costly be;   150
And drink thou up this deadly draught,
    Which I have brought to thee.

Then presently upon her knee
    Sweet Rosamond did fall;
And pardon of the queen she crav'd
    For her offences all.
Take pity on my youthful years,
    Fair Rosamond did cry;
And let me not with poison strong
    Enforced be to die.   160

I will renounce my sinful life,
    And in some cloister bide;
Or else be banish'd, if you please,
    To range the world so wide.
And, for the fault which I have done,
    Though I was forc'd thereto,
Preserve my life, and punish me
    As you think good to do.

And, with these words, her lily hands
    She wrung full often there;   170
And down along her lovely face
    Proceeded many a tear.

But nothing could this furious queen
    Therewith appeased be;
'The cup of deadly poison strong,
    As she sate on her knee,

She gave this comely dame to drink;
    Who took it in her hand,
And from her bended knee arose,
    And on her feet did stand: 180
And, casting up her eyes to heaven,
    She did for mercy call;
And, drinking up the poison strong,
    Her life she lost withall.

And, when that death through every limb
    Had show'd its greatest spite,
Her chiefest foes did plain confess
    She was a glorious wight.
Her body then they did entomb,
    When life was fled away,   190
At 'Godstow,' near to Oxford town,
    As may be seen this day.

        [*V.* 191. Woodstock.]

XXX.

THE LAMENTATION OF JANE SHORE*.

If Rosamond, that was so fair,
Had cause her sorrows to declare,
Then let Jane Shore with sorrow sing,
That was beloved of a king.
   Then wanton wives in time amend,
   For love and beauty will have end.

In maiden years my beauty bright
Was loved dear of lord and knight;
But yet the love that they requir'd,
It was not as my friends desir'd.   10

My parents they, for thirst of gain,
A husband for me did obtain;
And I, their pleasure to fulfil,
Was forc'd to wed against my will.

To Matthew Shore I was a wife,
Till lust brought ruin to my life;
And then my life I lewdly spent,
Which makes my soul for to lament.

In Lombard-street I once did dwell,
As London yet can witness well;   20
Where many gallants did behold
My beauty in a shop of gold.

---

* There is a different ballad upon this subject in " The garland of good-will."

I spread my plumes as wantons do,
Some sweet and secret friend to woo,
Because my love I did not find
Agreeing to my wanton mind.

At last my name in court did ring,
Into the ears of Englands king,
Who came and lik'd, and love requir'd,
But I made coy what he desir'd.

Yet mistress Blague, a neighbour near,
Whose friendship I esteemed dear,
Did say, it was a gallant thing
To be beloved of a king.

By her persuasions I was led
For to defile my marriage-bed,
And wrong my wedded husband Shore,
Whom I had lov'd ten years before.

In heart and mind I did rejoice,
That I had made so sweet a choice;
And therefore did my state resign,
To be king Edwards concubine.

From city then to court I went,
To reap the pleasures of content;
And had the joys that love could bring,
And knew the secrets of a king.

When I was thus advanc'd on high,
Commanding Edward with mine eye,
For mistress Blague I, in short space,
Obtain'd a living from his grace.

No friend I had, but, in short time,
I made unto promotion climb;
But yet, for all this costly pride,
My husband could not me abide.

His bed, though wronged by a king,
His heart with grief did deadly sting;
From England then he goes away,
To end his life beyond the sea.

He could not live to see his name
Impaired by my wanton shame;   60
Although a prince of peerless might
Did reap the pleasure of his right.

Long time I lived in the court,
With lords and ladies of great sort;
And when I smil'd all men were glad,
But when I mourn'd my prince grew sad.

But yet an honest mind I bore
To helpless people that were poor;
I still redress'd the orphans cry,
And sav'd their lives condemn'd to die.   70

I still had ruth on widows tears,
I succour'd babes of tender years;
And never look'd for other gain
But love and thanks for all my pain.

At last my royal king did die,
And then my days of woe grew nigh;
When crook-back Richard got the crown,
King Edwards friends were soon put down.

I then was punish'd for my sin,
That I so long had lived in; 80
Yea, every one that was his friend,
This tyrant brought to shameful end.

Then, for my lewd and wanton life,
That made a strumpet of a wife,
I penance did in Lombard-street,
In shameful manner in a sheet:

Where many thousands did me view,
Who late in court my credit knew;
Which made the tears run down my face,
To think upon my foul disgrace. 90

Not thus content, they took from me
My goods, my livings, and my fee;
And charg'd that none should me relieve
Nor any succour to me give.

Then unto mistress Blague I went,
To whom my jewels I had sent,
In hope thereby to ease my want,
When riches fail'd, and love grew scant.

But she denied to me the same,
When in my need for them I came; 100
To recompence my former love,
Out of her doors she did me shove.

So love did vanish with my state,
Which now my soul repents too late;
Therefore example take by me,
For friendship parts in poverty.

But yet one friend, among the rest,
Whom I before had seen distress'd,
And sav'd his life, condemn'd to die,
Did give me food to succour me: 110

For which, by law, it was decreed,
That he was hanged for that deed;
His death did grieve me so much more,
Than had I died myself therefore.

Then those to whom I had done good,
Durst not ' afford ' me any food;
Whereby in vain I begg'd all day,
And still in streets by night I lay.

My gowns, beset with pearl and gold,
Were turn'd to simple garments old;   120
My chains and gems, and golden rings,
To filthy rags and loathsome things.

Thus was I scorn'd of maid and wife,
For leading such a wicked life;
Both sucking babes, and children small,
Did make their pastime at my fall.

I could not get one bit of bread,
Whereby my hunger might be fed:
Nor drink, but such as channels yield,
Or stinking ditches in the field.   130

Thus, weary of my life, at length,
I yielded up my vital strength,

[*V.* 116. restore.]

Within a ditch of loathsome scent,
Where carrion dogs do much frequent.

The which now since my dying day,
Is Shoreditch call'd, as writers say*;
Which is a witness of my sin,
For being concubine to a king.

You wanton wives, that fall to lust,
Be you assur'd that god is just;   140
Whoredom shall not escape his hand,
Nor pride unpunish'd in this land.

If god to me such shame did bring,
That yielded only to a king,
How shall they scape that daily run
To practise sin with every 'one?'

You husbands, match not but for love,
Lest some disliking after prove;
Women, be warn'd, when you are wives,
What plagues are due to sinful lives: 150
    Then, maids and wives, in time amend,
    For love and beauty will have end.

---

* In this particular the fair penitent was egregiously misled; Shoreditch having existed, by that very name, for some hundreds of years before she was born.

[*V.* 146. man.]

XXXI.

TRUE LOVE REQUITED:

OR,

THE BAILIFFS DAUGHTER OF ISLINGTON*.

THERE was a youth and a well-beloved youth,
   And he was a squires son:
He loved the bailiffs daughter dear,
   That lived in Islington.

She was coy, and she would not believe
   That he did love her so,
No nor at any time she would
   Any countenance to him show.

But when his friends did understand
   His fond and foolish mind,   10
They sent him up to fair London,
   An apprentice for to bind.

And when he had been seven long years,
   ' And never his love could see: '
" Many a tear have I shed for her sake,
   When she little thought of me."

---

* Dr. Percy thinks that Islington [a village] in Norfolk is [probably] the place here meant.

[*V.* 14. His love he had not seen.]

All the maids of Islington,
   Went forth to sport and play,
All but the bailiffs daughter dear,
   She secretly stole away.   20

She put off her gown of grey,
   And put on her puggish attire,
She's up to fair London gone,
   Her true love to require.

As she went along the road,
   The weather being hot and dry,
There was she aware of her true love
   At length came riding by.

She stepp'd to him as red as any rose,
   Catching hold of his bridle-ring: 30
" Pray you, kind sir, give me one penny,
   To ease my weary limb."

" I prithee, sweet-heart, can'st thou tell me,
   Where that thou wast born?"
" At Islington, kind sir, said she,
   Where I have had many a scorn."

" I prithee, sweet-heart, can'st thou tell me,
   Whether thou dost know
The bailiffs daughter of Islington?"
   " She's dead, sir, long ago."   40

" Then will I sell my goodly steed,
   My saddle and my bow;
I will into some far country,
   Where no man doth me know."

> " O stay, o stay, thou goodly youth,
>   Here she standeth by thy side,
> She is alive, she is not dead,
>   And is ready to be thy bride."
>
> " O farewell grief, and welcome joy,
>   Ten thousand times ' therefore; '   50
> For now I have seen mine own true love,
>   That I thought I should have seen no more!"

XXXII.

THE KING OF FRANCE'S DAUGHTER.

BY THOMAS DELONEY.

The full title, in the old copies, is " An excellent ballad of a prince of Englands courtship to the king of Frances daughter, and how the prince was disasterously slain, and how the aforesaid princess was afterwards married to a Forrester."

The story of this ballad, dr. Percy thinks, is taken from an incident in the domestic history of Charles the bald, king of France. "His daughter Judith was betrothed to Ethelwulph, king of England; but before the marriage was consummated, Ethelwulph died, and she returned to France; whence she was carried off by Baldwyn, forester of Flanders; who after many crosses and difficulties, at length obtained the kings consent to their marriage, and was made earl of Flanders. This happened about *A. D.* 863." The anecdote is recorded by Fabian, and, perhaps, by Holinshed.

The ballad is in Deloneys *Garland of good will.*

> In the days of old,
>   When fair France did flourish,
>
>   [*V.* 50. and more.]

Stories plainly told,
    Lovers felt annoy:
The king a daughter had,
    Beauteous, fair, and lovely,
Which made her father glad,
    She was his only joy;
A prince from England came,
Whose deeds did merit fame,   10
    He woo'd her long, and lo, at last,
Look, what he did require,
She granted his desire;
    Their hearts in one were linked fast:
Which when her father proved,
Lord, how he was moved,
    And tormented in his mind!
He sought for to prevent them,
And to discontent them,
    Fortune crossed [these] lovers kind.   20

When these princes twain
    Were thus barr'd of pleasure,
Through the kings disdain,
    Which their joys withstood;
The lady lock'd up close
    Her jewels and her treasure,
Having no remorse,
    Of state and royal blood:
In homely poor array,
She went from court away,   30

  To meet her love and hearts delight:
Who in a forest great
Had taken up his seat,
  To wait her coming in the night:
But lo! what sudden danger
To this princely stranger
  Chanced as he sat alone!
By outlaws he was robbed,
And with poniard stabbed,
  Uttering many a dying groan.   40

The princess, armed by him,
  And by true desire,
Wandering all that night,
  Without dread at all;
Still unknown she pass'd,
  In her strange attire,
Coming at the last,
  Within echos call,
You fair woods, quoth she,
Honoured may you be,   50
  Harbouring my hearts delight:
Which doth encompass here,
My joy and only dear,
  My trusty friend and comely knight.
Sweet, I come unto thee,
Sweet, I come to woo thee,
  That thou may'st not angry be,
For my long delaying,

And thy courteous staying,
    Amends for all I'll make to thee.   60

Passing thus alone,
    Through the silent forest,
Many a grievous groan,
    Sounded in her ear;
Where she heard a man
    To lament the sorest
Chance that ever came;
    Forc'd by deadly strife,
Farewell, my dear, quoth he,
Whom I shall never see,   70
    For why my life is at an end;
For thy sweet sake I die,
Through villains cruelty,
    To show I am a faithful friend:
Here lie I a bleeding,
While my thoughts are feeding,
    On the rarest beauty found;
O hard hap that may be,
Little knows my lady,
    My heart blood lies on the ground.   80

With that he gave a groan,
    That did break asunder
All the tender strings
    Of his gentle heart;
She who knew his voice,
    At his tale did wonder,

All her former joys
   Did to grief convert:
Straight she ran to see,
Who this man should be,   90
   That so like her love did speak;
And found, when as she came,
Her lovely lord lay slain,
   Smear'd in blood, which life did break:
Which when she espied,
Lord, how sore she cried!
   Her sorrows could not counted be;
Her eyes like fountains running,
While she cried out, My darling,
   Would god that I had died for thee!   100

His pale lips, alas!
   Twenty times she kissed,
And his face did wash
   With her brinish tears;
Every bleeding wound,
   Her fair face bedewed,
Wiping off the blood
   With her golden hair:
Speak, my love, quoth she,
Speak, dear prince, to me.   110
   One sweet word of comfort give;
Lift up thy fair eyes,
Listen to my cries,
   Think in what great grief I live.

All in vain she sued,
All in vain she wooed,
   The prince's life was fled and gone,
There stood she still mourning,
Till the suns returning,
   And bright day was coming on.   120

In this great distress,
   Quoth this royal lady,
Who can now express,
   What will become of me?
To my fathers court
   Never will I wander,
But some service seek
   Where I may placed be.
Whilst she thus made her moan,
Weeping all alone,   130
   In this deep and deadly fear,
A forester, all in green,
Most comely to be seen,
   Ranging the wood, did find her there,
Round beset with sorrow;
Maid, quoth he, good morrow,
   What hard hap hath brought you here?
Harder hap did never
Chance to a maiden ever
   Here lies slain my brother dear.   140

Where might I be plac'd?
   Gentle forester, tell me;

Where might I procure
   A service in my need?
Pains I will not spare,
   But will do my duty;
Ease me of my care,
   Help my extreme need."
The forester, all amazed,
On her beauty gazed,   150
   Till his heart was set on fire;
If, fair maid, quoth he,
You will go with me,
   You shall have your hearts desire.
He brought her to his mother,
And, above all other,
   He set forth this maidens praise;
Long was his heart inflamed,
At length her love he gained,
   So fortune did his glory raise.   160

Thus unknown he match'd
   With the kings fair daughter,
Children seven he had
   Ere she to him was known;
But when he understood
   She was a royal princess,
By this means at last
   He shewed forth her fame;
He cloth'd his children then,
(Not like to other men,)   170

In party-colours strange to see,
The right side cloth of gold,
The left side to behold
   Of woolen cloth still framed he :
Men thereat did wonder,
Golden fame did thunder
   This strange deed in every place :
The king of France came thither,
Being pleasant weather,
   In the woods the hart to chase.   180

The children there did stand,
   As their mother willed,
Where the royal king
   Must of force come by;
Their mother richly clad
   In fair crimson velvet;
Their father all in grey,
   Most comely to the eye.
When this famous king,
Noting every thing,   190
   Did ask, how he durst be so bold
To let his wife to wear,
And deck his children there,
   In costly robes of pearl and gold.
The forester bold replied,
And the cause descried,
   And to the king he thus did say,
Well may they, by their mother,

Wear rich clothes with other,
   Being by birth a princess gay. 200
The king upon these words,
  Most heedfully beheld them,
Till a crimson blush
  His conceit did cross:
The more I look, quoth he,
  Upon thy wife and children,
The more I call to mind
  My daughter whom I lost.
I am that child, quoth she,
Falling on her knee, 210
   Pardon me, my sovereign liege.
The king perceiving this,
His daughter dear did kiss,
  Till joyful tears did stop his speech:
With his train he turned,
And with her sojourned;
   Straight he dubb'd her husband knight;
He made him earl of Flanders,
One of his chief commanders,
   Thus was sorrow put to flight. 220

XXXIII.

THE FAMOUS FLOWER OF SERVING-MEN;

OR,

THE LADY TURNED SERVING-MAN.

You beauteous ladies, great and small,
I write unto you one and all,
Whereby that you may understand
What I have suffer'd in this land.

I was by birth a lady fair,
My fathers chief and only heir,
But when my good old father died,
Then I was made a young knights bride.

And then my love built me a bower,
Bedeck'd with many a fragrant flower;   10
A braver bower you ne'er did see,
Than my true love did build for me.

But there came thieves late in the night,
They robb'd my bower, and slew my knight,
And after that my knight was slain,
I could no longer there remain.

My servant [s] all from me did fly,
In th' midst of my extremity,
And left me by myself alone,
With a heart more cold than any stone.   20

Yet, though my heart was full of care,
Heaven would not suffer me to despair,
Wherefore in haste I chang'd my name
From fair Elise to Sweet-William.

And therewithall I cut my hair,
And dress'd myself in mans attire,
My doublet, hose, and beaver hat,
And a golden band about my neck.

With a silver rapier by my side,
So like a gallant I did ride; 30
The thing that I delighted on,
It was to be a serving-man.

Thus in my sumptuous mans array,
I bravely rode along the way;
And at the last it chanced so,
That I to the kings court did go.

Then to the king I bow'd full low,
My love and duty for to show;
And so much favour I did crave,
That I a serving-mans place might have*. 40

Stand up, brave youth, the king replied,
Thy service shall not be denied;
But tell me first what thou canst do,
Thou shalt be fitted thereunto.

* In the subsequent stanzas, as in the old *Second part* of *George Barnwel*, the narrative changes from the first person to the third; although, in the present instance, the transition seems to be made by the original author.

Wilt thou be usher of my hall,
To wait upon my nobles all?
Or wilt thou be tapster of my wine,
To wait on me when I do dine?

Or wilt thou be my chamberlàin,
To make my bed both soft and fine? 50
Or wilt thou be one of my guard?
And I will give thee thy reward.

Sweet-William, with a smiling face,
Said to the king, If 't please your grace,
To show such favour unto me,
Your chamberlain I fain would be.

The king then did the nobles call,
To ask the counsel of them all;
Who gave consent Sweet-William he,
The kings own chamberlain should be. 60

Now mark what strange thing came to pass,
As the king one day a hunting was,
With all his lords and noble train,
Sweet-William did at home remain.

Sweet-William had no company then
With him at home, but an old man;
And when he saw the house was clear,
He took a lute which he had there;

Upon the lute Sweet-William play'd,
And to the same he sung and said, 70
With a sweet and noble voice,
Which made the old man to rejoice:

" My father was as brave a lord
As ever Europe did afford,
My mother was a lady bright,
My husband was a valiant knight.

And I myself a lady gay,
Bedeck'd with gorgeous rich array.
The bravest lady in the land
Had not more pleasure at command. 80

I had my music every day,
Harmonious lessons for to play;
I had my virgins fair and free,
Continually to wait on me.

But now, alas! my husband's dead,
And all my friends are from me fled;
My former joys are pass'd and gone,
For I am now a serving-man."

At last the king from hunting came,
And presently, upon the same, 90
He called for this good old man,
And thus to speak the king began:

What news, what news, old man? quoth he;
What news hast thou to tell to me?
Brave news, the old man he did say,
Sweet-William is a lady gay.

" If this be true thou tell'st to me
I'll make thee a lord of high degree;
But if thy words do prove a lie,
Thou shall be hang'd up presently."   100

But when the king the truth had found,
His joys did more and more abound:
According as the old man did say,
Sweet-William was a lady gay.

Therefore the king, without delay,
Put on her glorious rich array,
And upon her head a crown of gold,
Which was most famous to behold.

And then, for fear of further strife,
He took Sweet-William for his wife.   110
The like before was never seen
A serving-man to be a queen.

XXXIV.

THE CHILDREN IN THE WOOD;

OR,

THE NORFOLK GENTLEMANS LAST WILL AND TESTAMENT.

———appears to have been written in 1595, being entered in that year on the stationers books.

Now ponder well, you parents dear,
   The words which I shall write;
A doleful story you shall hear,
   In time brought forth to light:
A gentleman, of good account,
   In Norfolk liv'd of late,
Whose wealth and riches did surmount
   Most men of his estate.

Sore sick he was, and like to die,
   No help 'then' he could have;   10
His wife by him as sick did lie,
   And both possess'd one grave.
No love between these two was lost,
   Each was to other kind;
In love they lived, in love they died,
   And left two babes behind:

[*V.* 10. that.]

The one a fine and pretty boy,
    Not passing three years old:
The other a girl, more young than he,
    And made in beautys mould.
The father left his little son,
    As plainly doth appear,
When he to perfect age should come,
    Three hundred pounds a year;

And to his little daughter Jane
    Five hundred pounds in gold,
To be paid down on marriage-day,
    Which might not be controll'd:
But if the children chance to die
    Ere they to age should come,
Their uncle should possess their wealth,
    For so the will did run.

Now, brother, said the dying man,
    Look to my children dear;
Be good unto my boy and girl,
    No friends else I have here:
To god and you I do commend
    My children, night and day;
But little while, be sure, we have,
    Within this world to stay.

You must be father and mother both,
    And uncle, all in one;
God knows what will become of them,
    When I am dead and gone.

With that bespake their mother dear,
    O brother kind, quoth she,
You are the man must bring our babes
    To wealth or misery.

And if you keep them carefully,
    Then god will you reward;   50
If otherwise you seem to deal,
    God will your deeds regard.
With lips as cold as any stone,
    She kiss'd her children small:
" God bless you both, my children dear."
    With that the tears did fall.

These speeches then their brother spoke
    To this sick couple there:
The keeping of your children dear,
    Sweet sister do not fear;   60
God never prosper me nor mine,
    Nor ought else that I have,
If I do wrong your children dear,
    When you are laid in grave.

Their parents being dead and gone,
    The children home he takes,
And brings them home unto his house,
    And much of them he makes.
He had not kept these pretty babes
    A twelvemonth and a day,   70
But, for their wealth, he did devise
    To make them both away.

He bargain'd with two ruffians 'strong'
    Which were of furious mood,
That they should take 'these' children young,
    And slay them in a wood.
He told his wife, and all he had,
    He did the children send,
To be brought up in fair Londòn,
    With one that was his friend.   80

Away then went these pretty babes,
    Rejoicing at that tide,
Rejoicing with a merry mind,
    They should on cock-horse ride.
They prate and prattle pleasantly,
    As they rode on the way,
To those that should their butchers be,
    And work their lives decay.

So that the pretty speech they had,
    Made 'murders' hearts relent;   90
And they that undertook the deed
    Full sore they did repent.
Yet one of them, more hard of heart,
    Did vow to do his charge,
Because the wretch that hired him
    Had paid him very large.

    [*V*. 73. rude.]   [*V*. 75. the.]
    [*V*. 90. murderers.]

The other would not agree thereto,
    So here they fell at strife;
With one another they did fight,
    About the childrens life: 100
And he that was of mildest mood,
    Did slay the other there,
Within an unfrequented wood;
    While babes did quake for fear.

He took the children by the hand,
    When tears stood in their eye,
And bade them come and go with him,
    And look they did not cry:
And two long miles he led them on,
    While they for food complain: 110
Stay here, quoth he, I'll bring you bread,
    When I do come again.

These pretty babes, with hand in hand,
    Went wandering up and down;
But never more they saw the man,
    Approaching from the town:
Their pretty lips, with black-berries,
    Were all besmear'd and died,
And, when they saw the darksome night,
    They sate them down and cried.   120

Thus wander'd these two pretty babes,
    Till death did end their grief;
In one anothers arms they died,
    As babes wanting relief.

No burial these pretty babes
    Of any man receives,
Till Robin-red-breast, painfully,
    Did cover them with leaves.

And now the heavy wrath of god
    Upon their uncle fell;
Yea, fearful fiends did haunt his house,
    His conscience felt an hell.
His barns were fired, his goods consum'd,
    His lands were barren made,
His cattle died within the field,
    And nothing with him stay'd.

And, in the voyage of Portugal*,
    Two of his sons did die;
And, to conclude, himself was brought
    To extreme misery.
He pawn'd and mortgag'd all his land
    Ere seven years came about:
And now, at length, this wicked act
    Did by this means come out:

The fellow that did take in hand
    These children for to kill,
Was for a robbery judg'd to die,
    As was gods blessed will;

---

* A. D. 1588. See the catalogue of the Harleian MSS. No 167, (15). Dr. Percy, not knowing that the text alludes to a particular event, has altered it to " a voyage to Portugal."

Who did confess the very truth,
　　The which is here express'd :　　　150
Their uncle died while he, for debt,
　　In prison long did rest.

' You that executors be made,'
　　And overseers eke,
Of children that be fatherless,
　　And infants mild and meek,
Take you example by this thing,
　　And yield to each his right,
Lest god, with such like misery,
　　Your wicked minds requite.　　　160

XXXV.

GEORGE BARNWEL.

[THE FIRST PART.]

ALL youths of fair Englànd,
　　That dwell both far and near,
Regard my story that I tell,
　　And to my song give ear.

A London lad I was,
　　A merchants prentice bound,
My name George Barnwel, that did spend
　　My master many a pound.

[*V.* 153. All you that be executors made.]

Take heed of harlots then,
    And their enticing trains;   10
For by 'their' means I have been brought
    To hang alive in chains.

As I, upon a day,
    Was walking through the street,
About my masters business,
    I did a wanton meet.

A gallant dainty dame,
    And sumptuous in attire,
With smiling looks she greeted me,
    And did my name require.   20

Which when I had declar'd,
    She gave me then a kiss,
And said, if I would come to her,
    I should have more than this.

In faith, my boy, quoth she,
    Such news I can you tell,
As shall rejoice your very heart,
    Then come where I do dwell.

Fair mistress, then said I,
    If I the place may know,   30
This evening I will be with you,
    For I abroad must go.

        [*V.* 11. that.]

To gather 'money' in,
 That is my masters due:
And, ere that I do home return,
 I'll come and visit you.

Good Barnwel, then quoth she,
 Do thou to Shoreditch come,
And ask for mistress Milwood there,
 Next door unto *The gun*.   40

And trust me on my truth,
 If thou keep touch with me,
For thy friends sake, as my own heart,
 Thou shalt right welcome be.

Thus parted we in peace,
 And home I passed right;
Then went abroad and gathered in,
 By six o'clock at night,

An hundred pound and one:
 With bag under my arm   50
I went to mistress Milwoods house,
 And thought on little harm;

And knocking at the door;
 Straightway herself came down;
Rustling in most brave attire,
 Her hood and silken gown.

[*V.* 33. moneys.]

Who, through her beauty bright,
   So gloriously did shine,
That she amaz'd my 'dazzled' eyes,
   She seemed so divine.   60

She took me by the hand,
   And with a modest grace,
Welcome, sweet Barnwel, then quoth she,
   Unto this homely place.

Welcome ten thousand times,
   More welcome then my brother,
And better welcome, I protest,
   Than any one or other.

And seeing I have thee found
   As good as thy word to be,   70
A homely supper, ere thou part,
   Thou shalt take here with me.

O pardon me, quoth I,
   Fair mistress I you pray;
For why, out of my masters house
   So long I dare not stay:

Alas, good sir, she said,
   Are you so strictly tied,
You may not with your dearest friend
   One hour or two abide?   80

[*V*. 59. dazzling.]

Faith, then the case is hard;
　　If it be so, quoth she,
I would I were a prentice bound,
　　To live in house with thee.

Therefore my sweetest George,
　　List well what I do say,
And do not blame a woman much
　　Her fancy to bewray:

Let not affections force
　　Be counted lewd desire;　　　　　　90
Nor think it not immodesty,
　　I should thy love require.

With that she turn'd aside,
　　And with a blushing red,
A mournful motion she bewray'd,
　　By holding down her head.

A handkerchief she had,
　　All wrought with silk and gold:
Which she, to stay her trickling tears,
　　Against her eyes did hold.　　　　　100

This thing unto my sight
　　Was wond'rous rare and strange;
And in my mind and inward thought
　　It wrought a sudden change:

That I so hardy was,
   To take her by the hand;
Saying, Sweet mistress, why do you
   So sad and heavy stand?

Call me no mistress now,
   But Sarah, thy true friend,   110
Thy servant Sarah, honouring thee
   Until her life doth end.

If thou would'st here alledge,
   Thou art in years a boy;
So was Adonis, yet was he
   Fair Venus' love and joy.

Thus I, that ne'er before
   Of woman found such grace,
And seeing now so fair a dame
   Give me a kind embrace,   120

I supp'd with her that night,
   With joys that did abound;
And for the same paid presently
   In money twice three pound.

An hundred kisses then,
   For my farewell she gave;
Saying, Sweet Barnwel, when shall I
   Again thy company have?

Stay not too long, my dear;
   Sweet George, have me in mind.   130
Her words bewitch'd my childishness,
   She uttered them so kind:

So that I made a vow,
   Next Sunday without fail,
With my sweet Sarah once again
   To tell some pleasant tale.

When she heard me say so,
   The tears fell from her 'eye;'
O George, quoth she, if thou dost fail,
   Thy Sarah sure will die.   140

Though long, yet lo! at last,
   'Th' appointed' day was come,
That I must with my Sarah meet;
   Having a mighty sum

Of money in my hand,
   Unto her house went I,
Whereas my love upon her bed
   In saddest sort did lie.

What ails my hearts delight,
   My Sarah dear? quoth I;   150
Let not my love lament and grieve,
   Nor sighing, pine, and die.

[*V.* 129. O stay.]   [*V.* 142. The 'pointed.]

But tell me, dearest friend,
  What may thy woes amend,
And thou shalt seek no means of help,
  Though forty pound I spend.

With that she turn'd her head,
  And sickly thus did say,
Oh, my sweet George, my grief is great,
  Ten pounds I have to pay   160

Unto a cruel wretch;
  And god he knows, quoth she,
I have it not. Tush, rise, quoth 'I,'
  And take it here of me.

Ten pounds, nor ten times ten,
  Shall make my love decay.
Then from 'my' bag into her lap,
  'I' cast ten pound straightway.

All blithe and pleasant then,
  To banqueting 'we' go;   170
She proffered 'me' to lie with her,
  And said it should be so.

And after that same time,
  I gave her store of coin,
Yea, sometimes fifty pound at once,
  All which I did purloin.

    [*V.* 153. But tell to me my dearest friend.]
[*V.* 163. he.]   [*V.* 167. his.]   [*V.* 168. He.]
[*V.* 170. they.]   [*V.* 171. him.]

And thus I did pass on:
   Until my master then
Did call to have his reckoning in,
   Cast up among his men.   180

The which when as I heard,
   I knew not what to say:
For well I knew that I was out
   Two hundred pounds that day.

Then from my master straight
   I ran in secret sort;
And unto Sarah Milwood then
   My state I did report.

But how she us'd this youth,
   In this his extreme need,   190
The which did her necessity
   So oft with money feed;

The Second Part, behold,
   Shall tell it forth at large;
And shall a strumpets wily ways,
   With all her tricks discharge.

THE SECOND PART*.

Young Barnwel comes to thee,
    Sweet Sarah, my delight;
I am undone, except thou stand
    My faithful friend this night.   200

Our master to command accounts,
    Hath just occasion found;
And I am found behind the hand
    Almost two hundred pound:

And therefore knowing not
    What answer for to make,
And his displeasure to escape,
    My way to thee I take;

Hoping in this 'extreme'
    Thou wilt my succour be,   210
That for a time I may remain
    In safety here with thee.

---

* Throughout this " Second part " (except in a single instance) the metre of the first line of each stanza is, in the old editions, lengthened by a couple of syllables; which are, occasionally at least, a manifest interpolation. The person, also, is, for the most part, changed from the first to the third, with evident impropriety. Dr. Percy has, very ingeniously, and with the least possible violence, restored the measure, by ejecting the superfluous syllables; and given consistency to the whole, by a restoration of the proper person: And, as it is now highly improbable that any further ancient copy will be found, and those which exist are manifestly corrupt, it seemed perfectly justifiable to adopt the judicious emendations of this ingenious editor.

With that she knit her brows,
    And looking all aquoy,
Quoth she, what should I have to do
    With any 'prentice boy?

Seeing you have purloin'd
    Your masters goods away,
The case is bad, and therefore here
    I mean thou shalt not stay.   220

Sweetheart, I said, thou know'st
    That all which I did get,
I gave it, and did spend it all,
    Upon thee every whit.

I loved thee so well,
    Thou could'st not ask the thing,
But that I did, incontinent,
    The same unto thee bring.

Thou art a paltry jack,
    To charge me in this sort,   230
Being a woman of credit good,
    And known of good report:

Therefore I tell thee flat,
    Be packing with good speed;
I do defy thee from my heart,
    And scorn thy filthy deed.

Is this the friendship, which
    Thou did'st to me ' profess? '
Is this the great affection which
    You seemed to express? 240

Fie on deceitful ' shrews! '
    The best is, I may speed
To get a lodging any where
    For money in my need.

False woman, now farewell,
    While twenty pound doth last,
My anchor in some other haven
    I will with wisdom cast.

' Perceiving by my words '
    That ' I ' had money store, 250
That she had gall'd ' me ' in such sort,
    It griev'd her heart full sore:

To call ' me ' back again
    She did suppose it best;
Stay, George, quoth she, thou art too quick;
    Why, man, I do but jest.

Think'st thou for all my speech,
    That I would let thee go?
Faith no, quoth she, my love to thee,
    I wis, is more than so. 260

[*V.* 238. protest. O. CC.]   [*V.* 241. shows.]

You will not deal with boys,
    I heard you even now swear,
Therefore I will not trouble you.
    ' Nay,' George, hark in thine ear:

Thou shalt not go to-night,
    What chance soe'er befall:
But, man, we'll have a bed for thee,
    Or else the devil take all.

Thus I, that was bewitch'd,
    And snared with fancy still,   270
Had not the power to 'get' away,
    Or to withstand her will.

Then wine ' on ' wine I call'd,
    And cheer upon good cheer;
And nothing in the world I thought,
    For Sarahs love too dear,

Whilst in her company,
    In joy and merriment;
' All ' all too little I did think,
    That I upon her spent.   280

A fig for careful thoughts!
    When all my gold is gone,
In faith, my girl, we will have more,
    Whoever it light upon.

[*V.* 264. My.]   [*V.* 271. put.]   [*V.* 279. and.]

My father's rich, why then,
 Should I want any gold?
With a father, indeed, quoth she,
 A son may well be bold.

I have a sister wed,
 I'll rob her ere I'll want.   290
Why then, quoth Sarah, they may well
 Consider of your scant.

Nay, I an uncle have,
 At Ludlow he doth dwell:
He is a grazier, which in wealth
 Doth all the rest excell.

Ere I will live in lack,
 And have no coin for thee;
I'll rob his house, and murder him.
 Why should you not? quoth she: 300

Were I a man, ere I
 Would live in poor estate;
On father, friends, and all my kin,
 I would my talons grate.

For without money, George,
 A man is but a beast:
And bringing money, thou shalt be
 Always my chiefest guest.

For say thou 'art' pursued
   With twenty hues and cries,   310
And with a warrant searched for,
   With Argus' hundred eyes:

Yet in my house 'thou 'rt' safe;
   Such privy ways there be,
That if they sought an hundred years,
   They could not find out thee*.

Carousing in their cups,
   Their pleasures to content,
George Barnwel had, in little space,
   His money wholly spent.   320

Which done, to Ludlow then
   He did provide to go,
To rob his wealthy uncle 'there,'
   His minion would it so.

And once he thought to take
   His father by the way;
But that he thought his master had
   Took order for his stay.

---

* After this stanza, the narrative is, uniformly, in the third person: owing, it may be imagined, to the authors inadvertency: as Barnwel, at the very outset, says

      "I have been brought
   To hang alive in chains."

'Unto' his uncle then
    He rode with might and main,   330
Where with welcome and good cheer
    He did him entertain.

A se'nnights space he stay'd,
    Until it chanced so,
His uncle with his cattle did
    Unto a market go.

His kinsman rode with him;
    And when he saw right plain,
Great store of money he had took,
    In coming home again,   340

Sudden, within a wood,
    He struck his uncle down,
And beat his brains out of his head;
    So sore he crack'd his crown;

And fourscore pound, in coin,
    Out of his purse he took;
And coming in to London town,
    The country quite forsook.

To Sarah then he came,
    Shewing his store of gold;   350
And how he had his uncle slain,
    To her he plainly told.

Tush, it's no matter, George,
  So we the money have,
To have good cheer in jolly sort,
  And deck us fine and brave.

They lived in filthy sort,
  Till all his store was gone:
And means to get them any more,
  I wis poor George had none.   360

Therefore, in railing sort,
  She thrust him out of door:
Which is the just reward they get,
  That spend upon a whore.

Oh! do me not disgrace,
  In this my need, quoth he.
She call'd him thief and murderer,
  With all despite might be.

The constable she sent,
  To have him apprehended;   370
And shew'd, in each degree, how far
  He had the law offended.

When Barnwel saw her drift*,
  To sea he got straightway;
Where fear, and dread, and conscience-sting,
  Upon himself doth stay.

* In this single stanza of the present part the measure of the old copies is, as here, correct.

Unto the mayor then,
   He did a letter write;
Wherein his own and Sarahs faults
   He did at large recite.   380

She apprehended was,
   And then to Ludlow sent:
Where she was judg'd, condemn'd, and hang'd,
   For murder, incontinent.

And there this quean did die,
   This was her greatest gains:
For murder, in Polonia,
   Was Barnwel hang'd in chains.

Lo! here's the end of youth,
   That after harlots haunt;   390
Who, in the spoil of other men,
   About the streets do flaunt.

XXXVI.

KING HENRY THE SECOND AND THE MILLER OF MANSFIELD.

[THE FIRST PART.]

HENRY our royal king, would ride a hunting,
   To the green forest, so pleasant and fair;
To have the hart chased, and dainty does tripping;
   Untò merry Sherwood his nobles repair:

Hawk and hound was unbound, all things prepar'd
For the same, to the game, with good regard.

All a long summers day rode the king pleasantly,
   With all his princes and nobles each one;
Chasing the hart and hind, and the buck gallantly,
   · Till the dark evening enforc'd them turn home.   10
Then at last, riding fast, he had lost quite
All his lords in the wood, late in dark night.

Wandering thus wearily, all alone, up and down,
   With a rude miller he met at the last;
Asking the ready way unto fair Nottingham,
   Sir, quoth the miller, your way you have lost:
Yet I think what I think, truth for to say,
You do not likely ride out of your way.

Why, what dost thou think of me? quoth our king
      merrily,
   Passing thy judgement upon me so brief.   20
Good faith, quoth the miller, I mean not to flatter thee;
   I guess thee to be but some gentleman thief:
Stand thee back, in the dark; light thee not down,
Lest that I presently crack thy knaves crown.

Thou dost abuse me much, quoth our king, saying thus:
   I am a gentleman; lodging I lack.
Thou hast not, quoth the miller, one groat in thy purse:
   All thy inheritance hangs on thy back.
" I have gold to discharge all that I call;
If it be forty pence, I will pay all."   30

If thou beest a true man, then said the miller,
  I swear by my toll-dish, I'll lodge thee all night.
Here's my hand, quoth the king, that was I ever.
  Nay, soft, quoth the miller, thou may'st be a sprite:
Better I'll know thee, ere hands I do take;
With none but honest men hands will I shake.

Thus they went all along unto the millers house,
  Where they were seething of puddings and souse:
The miller first enter'd in, then after him the king;
  Never came he in so smoky a house.   40
Now, quoth he, let me see here what you are.
Quoth our king, Look your fill, and do not spare.

" I like well thy countenance, thou hast an honest face;
  With my son Richard this night thou shalt lie."
Quoth his wife, By my troth, it is a handsome youth;
  Yet it is best, husband, for to deal warily:
Art thou not a run-away, I pray thee, youth, tell?
Show me thy passport, and all shall be well.

Then our king presently, making low courtesy,
  With his hat in his hand, thus he did say: 50
I have no passport, nor never was servitor;
  But a poor courtier, rode out of my way:
And for your kindness here offered to me,
I will requite it in every degree.

Then to the miller his wife whisper'd secretly,
  Saying, It seems, this youth's of good kin,
Both by his apparel, and eke by his manners;
  To turn him out, certainly 'twere a great sin.

Yea, quoth he, you may see, he hath some grace,
When he doth speak to his betters in place.   60

Well, quoth the millers wife, young man, welcome here,
   And, though I say it, well lodg'd thou shalt be:
Fresh straw I will have laid on thy bed so brave,
   Good brown hempen sheets likewise, quoth she,
Ay, quoth the good man; and when that is done,
You shall lie with no worse than our own son.

Nay, first, quoth Richard, good fellow, tell me true;
   Hast any creepers within thy gay hose?
Or art thou not troubled with the scabado?
   I pray you, quoth the king, what things are those? 70
Art thou not lousy, nor scabby? quoth he;
If thou be'st, surely thou liest not with me.

This caus'd the king suddenly to laugh most heartily,
   Till the tears trickled down from his eyes.
Then to their supper were they set orderly,
   With a hot bag-pudding, and good apple-pies;
Nappy ale, stout and stale, in a brown bowl,
Which did about the board merrily troul.

Here, quoth the miller, good fellow, I drink to thee,
   And to all courtnols that courteous be.   80
I'll pledge you, quoth our king, and thank you heartily,
   For your good welcome in every degree;
And here, in like manner, I'll drink to your son.
Do so, quoth Richard; but quick let it come.

Wife, quoth the miller, fetch me forth Lightfoot,
   That we of his sweetness a little may taste:
A fair venison pasty, then brought she forth presently;
   Eat, quoth the miller; but, sir, make no waste.
Here's dainty lightfoot, in faith, said our king;
I never before eat so dainty a thing.   90

I wis, said Richard, no dainty at all it is,
   For we do eat of it every day.
In what place, said our king, may be bought like to
   this?
We never pay a penny for it, by my fay:
From merry Sherwood we fetch it home here;
Now and then we make bold with our kings deer.

Then I think, said our king, that it is venison.
   Each fool, quoth Richard, full well may see that:
Never are we without two or three under the roof,
   Very well flesh'd, and excellent fat: 100
But, pray thee, say nothing where'er thou dost go;
We would not, for two-pence, the king should it
   know.

Doubt not, then said our king, my promis'd secrecy;
   The king shall never know more on't for me.
A cup of lambswool they drank unto him then,
   And to their beds they pass'd presently.
The nobles, next morning, went all up and down,
For to seek out the king in every town.

At last, at the millers house, soon they espied him plain,
    As he was mounting upon his fair steed;   110
To whom they came presently, falling down on their
    knees;
Which made the millers heart woefully bleed:
Shaking and quaking before him he stood,
Thinking he should have been hang'd, by the rood.

The king perceiving him fearful and trembling,
    Drew forth his sword, but nothing he said:
The miller down did fall, crying before them all,
    Doubting the king would have cut off his head:
But his kind courtesy there to requite,
Gave him a living and made him a knight.   120

THE SECOND PART.

When as our royal king came home from Nottingham,
    And with his nobles at Westminster lay;
Recounting the sports and pastimes they had ta'en,
    In this late progress along by the way;
Of them all, great and small, he did protest,
The miller of Mansfields sport liked him best.

And now, my lords, quoth the king, I am determined,
    Against Saint Georges next sumptuous feast,
That this old miller, our last confirmed knight,
    With his son Richard, shall both be my guest: 130
For, in this merriment, 'tis my desire,
To talk with the jolly knight, and the brave squire.

When as the noblemen saw the kings pleasantness,
  They were right joyful and glad in their hearts;
A pursuivant there was sent straight on the business,
  The which had many times been in those parts.
When he came to the place where he did dwell,
His message orderly then he did tell.

God save your worship, then said the messenger,
  And grant your lady her [own] hearts desire, 140
And to your son Richard good fortune and happiness,
  That sweet young gentleman, and gallant young squire;
Our king greets you all, and thus doth say,
You must come to the court on Saint Georges day:

Therefore, in any case, fail not to be in place.
  I wis, quoth the miller, this is an odd jest:
What should we do there? he said: faith, I am half afraid.
  I doubt, quoth Richard, be hang'd at the least.
Nay, quoth the messenger, you do mistake;
Our king he prepares a great feast for your sake. 150

Then said the miller, Now, by my troth, messenger,
  Thou hast contented my worship full well;
Hold, here's three farthings, to quit thy great gentleness,
  For these happy tidings which thou dost tell:
Let me see, hear'st thou me? tell to our king,
We'll wait on his mastership in every thing.

The pursuivant smiled at their simplicity,
   And, making many legs, took their reward:
And, taking then his leave with great humility,
   To the kings court again he repair'd;   160
Shewing unto his grace, in each degree,
The knights most liberal gift and bounty.

When as he was gone away, thus did the miller say:
   Here comes expences and charges indeed;
Now we must needs be brave, though we spend all we have;
   For of new garments we have great need:
Of horses and serving-men we must have store,
With bridles and saddles, and twenty things more.

Tush, sir John, quoth his wife, neither do fret nor frown;
   You shall be at no more charges for me,   170
For I will turn and trim up my old russet gown,
   With every thing as fine as may be;
And on our mill-horses full swift we will ride,
With pillows and pannels, as we shall provide.

In this most stately sort, rode they unto the court,
   Their jolly son Richard foremost of all;
Who set up, by good hap, a cocks feather in his cap;
   And so they jetted down towards the kings hall:
The merry old miller, with his hand on his side;
His wife, like maid Marian, did mince at that tide. 180

The king and his nobles, that heard of their coming,
　Meeting this gallant knight, with his brave train;
Welcome, sir knight, quoth he, with this your gay lady;
　Good sir John Cockle, once welcome again:
And so is the squire, of courage so free,
Quoth Dick, A bots on you, do you know me?

Quoth our king gently, How should I forget thee?
　Thou wast mine own bed fellow, well that I wot.
" But I do think on a trick."—" Tell me that, prithee
　　Dick."
" How we with farting did make the bed hot." 190
Thou whoreson, happy knave, then quoth the knight,
Speak cleanly to our king, or else go s——.

The king and his counsellors heartily laugh'd at this,
　While the king took them both by the hand;
With ladies and their maids, like to the Queen of
　　Spades,
　The millers wife did so orderly stand:
A milk-maids curtesy at every word;
And down the folks were set at the side-board:

Where the king royally, in princely majesty,
　Sate at his dinner with joy and delight:　　200
When he had eaten well, to jesting then 'he' fell,
　Taking a bowl of wine, drank to the knight:
Here's to you both, he said, in wine, ale and beer;
Thanking you all for your country cheer.

Quoth sir John Cockle, I'll pledge you a pottle,
   Were it the best ale in Nottinghamshire:
But, then said our king, I do think of a thing;
   Some of your lightfoot I would we had here.
Ho, ho, quoth Richard, full well I may say it,
'Tis knavery to eat it, and then to bewray it.   210

Why art thou angry? quoth our king merrily;
   In faith, I take it very unkind:
I thought thou would'st pledge me in ale and wine
      heartily.
   Y' are like to stay, quoth Dick, till I have din'd:
You feed us with twattling dishes so small;
Zounds, a black-pudding is better than all.

Ay, marry, quoth our king, that were a dainty thing,
   If a man could get one here for to eat,
With that Dick straight arose, and pluck'd one out of
      his hose,
   Which with heat of his breach began to sweat. 220
The king made a proffer to snatch it away:
"'Tis meat for your master: good sir, you must stay."

Thus with great merriment, was the time wholly spent;
   And then the ladies prepared to dance:
Old sir John Cockle, and Richard, incontinent,
   Unto 'their places' the king did advance:
Here with the ladies such sport they did make,
The nobles with laughing did make their 'sides' ake.

    [*V.* 226. this practice.]   [*V.* 228. hearts.]

Many thanks for their pains did the king give them then,
    Asking young Richard, if he would wed: 230
" Among those ladies free, tell me which liketh thee."
    Quoth he, Jug Grumball, with the red head:
She's my love, she's my life, she will I wed;
She hath sworn I shall have her maidenhead.

Then sir John Cockle the king called unto him,
    And of merry Sherwood made him o'erseer;
And gave him out of hand three hundred pound yearly;
    " But now take heed you steal no more of my deer:
And once a quarter let's here have your view;
And thus, sir John Cockle, I bid you adieu."

XXXVII.

KING JOHN AND THE ABBOT OF CANTERBURY.

All the old impressions of this ballad, hitherto met with, are miserably corrupt; but dr. Percy, having found a copy of it in his folio MS., some palpable omissions are now supplied upon the authority of the *Reliques*.

The same story is related of a king and an abbot in *El Patrañuelo de Juan Timoneda* (a collection of Spanish novels) Alcala, 1576, being there taken, it is probable, from some older authority: possibly, *Novella IV. di Sacchetti*, which Timoneda might have met with in MS.

I'll tell you a story, a story anon,
Of a noble prince, and his name was king John;
For he was a prince, and a prince of great might,
He held up great wrongs, and he put down great right.
        Derry down, down, hey derry down.

I'll tell you a story, a story so merry,
Concerning the abbot of Canterbury,
And of his house keeping and high renown,
Which made him repair to fair London town.
      Derry down, &c.

" How now, brother abbot! 'tis told unto me,
That thou keepest a far better house than I;   10
And for thy house keeping and high renown,
I fear thou hast treason against my crown."
      Derry down, &c.

" I hope, my liege, that you owe me no grudge,
For spending of my true gotten goods."
" If thou dost not answer me questions three,
Thy head shall be taken from thy body."
      Derry down, &c.

" When I am set ' so high on my steed,'
With my crown of gold upon my head,
Amongst all my nobility, with joy and much mirth,
Thou must tell me to one penny what I am worth. 20
      Derry down, &c.

And the next question ' thou ' must not flout,
How long I shall be riding the world about;
And [at] the third question thou must not shrink,
But tell to me truly what I do think."
      Derry down, &c.

' O these are hard questions for my shallow wit,
For I cannot answer your grace as yet,

But if you will give me but three days space,
I'll do my endeavour to answer your grace."
Derry down, &c.

" O three days space I will thee give,
For that is the longest day thou hast to live;   30
And if thou dost not answer these questions right,
Thy head shall be taken from thy body quite."
Derry down, &c.

And as the old shepherd was going to his fold,
He spied the old abbot come riding along,
" How now, master abbot! you're welcome home:
What news have you brought us from good king John?"
Derry down, &c.

" Sad news, sad news, I have thee to give,
For I have but three days space to live;
If I do not answer him questions three,
My head will be taken from my body.   40
Derry down, &c

When he is set ' so high on his steed,'
With his crown of gold upon his head,
Amongst all his nobility, with joy and much mirth,
I must tell him to one penny what he is worth.
Derry down, &c.

And the next question I must not flout,
How long he shall be riding the world about;
And [at] the third question I must not shrink,
But tell him truly what he does think."
Derry down, &c.

" O master, did you never hear it yet,
That a fool may learn a wise man wit;   50
Lend me but your horse and your apparel,
I'll ride to fair London and answer the quarrel."
                              Derry down, &c.

" Now I am set 'so high on my steed,'
With my crown of gold upon my head,
Amongst all my nobility, with joy and much mirth,
Now tell me, to one penny, what I am worth."
                              Derry down, &c.

" For thirty pence our saviour was sold,
Amongst the false Jews, as I have been told,
And nine and twenty's the worth of thee,
For I think thou art one penny worser than he."   60
                              Derry down, &c.

[The king he laugh'd and swore by Saint Bittel
I did not think I had been worth so little.]
" 'At' the next question thou mayest not flout,
How long I shall be riding the world about."
                              [Derry down, &c.]

" You must rise with the sun and ride with the same
Until the next morning he rises again;
And then I am sure, you will make no doubt,
But in twenty-four hours you'll ride it about."
                              Derry down, &c.

[The king he laugh'd, and swore by Saint John,
I did not think it could be gone so soon.]   70

" And [at] the third question thou must not shrink,
But tell to me truly what I do think."
>[Derry down, &c.]

" All that I can do, and 'twill make your grace merry,
For you think I'm the abbot of Canterbury;
But I'm his poor shepherd, as [here] you may see,
And am come to beg pardon for 'him' and for me."
>Derry down, &c.

The king he turn'd him about and did smile,
Saying, thou shall be the abbot the other while.
" O no, my 'liege,' there is no such need,
For I can neither write nor read." 80
>Derry down, &c.

" Then four pounds a week will I give unto thee,
For this merry true jest thou hast told unto me;
And tell the old abbot when thou comest home,
Thou hast brought him a pardon from good king John."
>Derry down, &c.

XXXVIII.

SIR LANCELOT DU LAKE.

BY THOMAS DELONEY.

The title of the old copies is, but very improperly, " The noble atchievements of king Arthur, and his knights of the round table. To the tune of Flying Fame." The two first lines of this ballad are sung by Falstaff in the second part of K. Henry IV. It is inserted in " The garland of good will."

WHEN Arthur first in court began,
   And was approved king;
By force of arms great victories won,
   And conquest home did bring;

Then into Britain straight he came,
   Where fifty good and able
Knights then repaired unto him,
   Which were of the Round Table.

And many justs and tournaments
   Before him there were prest,   10
Wherein these knights did then excell,
   And far surmount the rest.

But one sir Lancelot du Lake,
   Who was approved well,
He, in his fights and deeds of arms,
   All others did excell.

When he had rested him a while,
    To play, and game, and sport;
He thought he would approve himself
    In some advent'rous sort: 20

He armed rode in forest wide,
    And met a damsel fair,
Who told him of adventures great;
    Whereto he gave good ear.

Why should not I? quoth Lancelot tho,
    For that cause came I hither.
Thou seem'st, quoth she, a knight right good,
    And I will bring thee thither,

Whereas the mightiest knight doth dwell,
    That now is of great fame: 30
Wherefòre tell me what knight thou art;
    And then what is thy name.

" My name is Lancelot du Lake."
    Quoth she, It likes me, then;
Here dwells a knight that never was
    O'ermatch'd of any man;

Who hath in prison threescore knights
    And four, that he hath bound;
Knights of king Arthurs court they be,
    And of the Table Round.   40

She brought him to a river then,
    And also to a tree,
'Whereon' a copper bason hung,
    'And many' shields to see.

He struck so hard, the bason broke:
    When Tarquin heard the sound,
He drove a horse before him straight,
    Whereon a knight was bound.

Sir knight, then said sir Lancelot,
    Bring me that horse-load hither,   50
And lay him down, and let him rest;
    We'll try our force together:

For, as I understand, thou hast,
    As far as thou art able,
Done great despite and shame unto
    The knights of the Round Table.

If thou art of the Table Round,
    Quoth Tarquin speedily,
Both thee, and all thy fellowship,
    I utterly defy.   50

That's over much, quoth Lancelot tho;
    Defend thee by and by.
They put their spurs unto their steeds,
    And each at other fly.

    [*V*. 43. Whereas.]   [*V*. 44. His fellows.]

They couch'd their spears, and horses run,
   As though they had been thunder;
And each struck then upon the shield,
   Wherewith they brake asunder.

Their horses backs brake under them;
   The knights they were astound:
To avoid their horses they made haste
   To light upon the ground.

They took them to their shields full fast,
   Their swords they drew out then;
With mighty strokes most eagerly
   Each one at other run.

They wounded were, and bled full sore,
   For breath they both did stand;
And leaning on their swords a while,
   Quoth Tarquin, Hold thy hand;

And tell to me what I shall ask.
   Say on, quoth Lancelot tho.
Thou art, quoth Tarquin, the best knight
   That ever I did know;

And like a knight that I did hate:
   So that thou be not he,
I will deliver all the rest,
   And eke accord with thee.

That is well said, quoth Lancelot then;
   But sith it so must be,   90
What is the knight thou hatest thus,
   I pray thee show to me?

His name is Lancelot du Lake;
   He slew my brother dear;
Him I suspect of all the rest:
   I would I had him here.

" Thy wish thou hast, but ' yet ' unknown;
   I am Lancelot du Lake,
Now knight of Arthurs Table Round,
   King Hands son of Benwake: 100

And I defy thee, do thy worst."
   Ha, ha, quoth Tarquin tho,
One of us two shall end our lives,
   Before that we do go.

If thou be Lancelot du Lake,
   Then welcome shalt thou be;
Wherefore see thou thyself defend,
   For now I dèfy thee.

They hurled then together fast,
   Like two wild boars so rashing,   110
And with their swords and shields they ran
   At one another, slashing.

     [*V.* 100. "King Hauds son of Schuwake."]

The ground besprinkled was with blood,
  Tarquin began to faint;
For he had back'd, and bore his shield
  So low, he did repent.

Which soon espied Lancelot tho;
  He leap'd upon him then,
He pull'd him down upon his knee,
  And rushed off his helm;   120

And then [he] struck his neck in two:
  And, when he had done so,
From prison threescore knights and four
  Lancelot deliver'd tho.

XXXIX.

SIR GUY OF WARWICK.

The full title is, "A pleasant song of the valiant deeds of chivalry atchieved by that noble knight, sir Guy of Warwick, who for the love of Fair Phillis became a hermet, and died in a cave of a craggy rock a mile distant from Warwick. Tune, *Was ever man*, &c." This ballad was entered on the Stationers books 5th January 1591-2.

Was ever knight, for ladys sake,
  So toss'd in love, as I, sir Guy,
For Phillis fair, that lady bright
  As ever man beheld with eye?

She gave me leave myself to try,
   The valiant knight with shield and spear,
Ere that her love she would grant me;
   Which made me venture far and near.

The proud sir Guy, a baron bold,
   In deeds of arms the doughty knight,   10
That every day in England was,
   With sword and spear in field to fight;
An English man I was by birth,
   In faith of Christ a Christian true;
The wicked laws of infidels
   I sought by 'prowess' to subdue.

'Nine' hundred twenty years, and odd
   After our saviour Christ his birth,
When king Athèlstan wore the crown,
   I lived here upon the earth.   20
Sometime I was of Warwick earl,
   And, as I said, on very truth,
A ladys love did me constrain
   To seek strange ventures in my youth:

To try my fame by feats of arms,
   In strange and sundry heathen lands;
Where I atchieved, for her sake,
   Right dangerous conquests with my hands.
For first I sail'd to Normandy,
   And there I stoutly won in fight,   30
The emperours daughter of Almain,
   From many a valiant worthy knight.

    [*V*. 16. power.]   [*V*. 17. Two.]

Then passed I the seas of Greece,
   To help the emperour to his right,
Against the mighty soldans host
   Of puissant Persians for to fight:
Where I did slay of Saracens,
   And heathen pagans, many a man,
And slew the soldans cousin dear,
   Who had to name, doughty Colbròn.   40

Ezkeldered, that famous knight,
   To death likewise I did pursue,
And Almain, king of Tyre, also,
   Most terrible in fight to view:
I went into the soldans host,
   Being thither on ambassage sent,
And brought away his head with me,
   I having slain him in his tent.

There was a dragon in the land,
   Most fiercely met me by the way,   50
As he a lion did pursue,
   Which I also myself did slay.
From thence I pass'd the seas of Greece,
   And came to Pavy land aright,
Where I the duke of Pavy kill'd,
   His heinous treason to requite.

And after came into this land,
   Towards fair Phillis, lady bright;
For love of whom I travel'd far,
   To try my manhood and my might.   60

But when I had espoused her,
  I stay'd with her but forty days,
But there I left this lady fair,
  And then I went beyond the seas.

All clad in gray, in pilgrim sort,
  My voyage from her I did take,
Unto ' the ' blessed holy land,
  For Jesus Christ my saviours sake:
Where I earl Jonas did redeem,
  And all his sons, which were fifteen,
Who, with the cruel Saracen,
  In prison, for long time, had been.

I slew the giant Amarant,
  In battle fiercely hand to hand:
And doughty Barknard killed I,
  The mighty duke of that same land.
Then I to England came again,
  And here with Colbron fell I fought,
An ugly giant, which the Danes
  Had for their champion hither brought.

I overcame him in the field,
  And slew him dead right valiantly;
Where I the land did then redeem
  From Danish tribute utterly;
And afterwards I offered up
  The use of weapons solemnly,
At Winchester, whereas I fought,
  In sight of many far and nigh.

[*V.* 67. that.]

In Windsor-forest I did slay
   A boar of passing might and strength;   90
The like in England never was,
   For hugeness, both in breadth and length.
Some of his bones in Warwick, yet,
   Within the castle there, do lie;
One of his shield-bones, to this day,
   Hangs in the city of Coventry.

On Dunsmore-heath I also slew
   A monstrous, wild, and cruel beast,
Call'd the dun-cow of Dunsmore-heath;
   Which many people had oppress'd: 100
Some of her bones in Warwick, yet,
   Still for a monument 'do' lie;
Which, unto every lookers view,
   As wond'rous strange, they may espy.

Another dragon in the land,
   I also did in fight destroy,
Which did both men and beasts oppress,
   And all the country sore annoy.
And then to Warwick came again,
   Like pilgrim poor, and was not known,   110
And there I liv'd a hermits life,
   A mile and more out of the town.

Where, with my hand, I hew'd a house,
   Out of a craggy rock of stone;
And lived like a palmer poor,
   Within that cave, myself alone;

[*V.* 102. doth.]

And dayly came to beg my food
   Of Phillis, at my castle-gate,
Not known unto my loving wife,
   Who dayly mourned for her mate. 120

Till at the last I fell sore sick,
   Yea, sick so sore that I must die;
I sent to her a ring of gold,
   By which she knew me presently.
Then she repaired to the cave,
   Before that I gave up the ghost;
Herself clos'd up my dying eyes:
   My Phillis fair, whom I lov'd most.

Thus dreadful Death did me arrest,
   To bring my corpse unto the grave; 130
And like a palmer died I,
   Whereby I 'hoped' my soul to save.
My body in Warwick yet doth lie,
   Though now it is consum'd to mold;
My 'statue as' engraven in stone,
   This present day you may behold.

   [*V*. 132. hope.]   [*V*. 135. stature was.]

XL.

THE HONOUR OF A LONDON PRENTICE.

Of a worthy London prentice
 My purpose is to speak,
And tell his brave adventures,
 Done for his countrys sake:
Seek all the world about,
 And you shall hardly find
A man in valour to exceed
 A prentice' gallant mind.

He was born [and bred] in Cheshire,
 The chief of men was he,   10
From thence brought up to London,
 A prentice for to be.
A merchant on the bridge
 Did like his service so,
That, for three years, his factor
 To Turkey he should go.

And in that famous country
 One year he had not been,
Ere he by tilt maintained
 The honour of his queen;   20
Elizabeth his princess
 He nobly did make known,
To be the phœnix of the world,
 And none but she alone.

In armour richly gilded,
    Well mounted on a steed,
One score of knights most hardy
    One day he made to bleed;
And brought them all to ground,
    Who proudly did deny   30
Elizabeth to be the pearl
    Of princely majesty.

The king of that same country
    Thereat began to frown,
And will'd his son, there present,
    To pull this youngster down;
Who, at his fathers words,
    These boasting speeches said,
Thou art a traitor, English boy,
    And hast the traitor play'd.   40

" I am no boy, nor traitor,
    Thy speeches I defy,
For which I'll be revenged
    Upon thee, by and by;
A London prentice still
    Shall prove as good a man,
As any of your Turkish knights,
    Do all the best you can."

And therewithall he gave him
    A box upon the ear,   50
Which broke his neck asunder,
    As plainly doth appear.

Now know, proud Turk, quoth he,
   I am no English boy,
That can, with one small box o' th' ear,
   The prince of Turks destroy.

When as the king perceived
   His son so strangely slain,
His soul was sore afflicted,
   With more than mortal pain;   60
And, in revenge thereof,
   He swore that he should die
The cruel'st death that ever man
   Beheld with mortal eye.

Two lions were prepared
   This prentice to devour,
Near famish'd up with hunger,
   Ten days within a tower,
To make them far more fierce,
   And eager of their prey,   70
To glut themselves with human gore
   Upon this dreadful day.

The appointed time of torment
   At length grew nigh at hand,
Where all the noble ladies
   And barons of the land
Attended on the king,
   To see this prentice slain,
And buried in the hungry maws
   Of those fierce lions twain.   80

Then in his shirt of cambric,
   With silk most richly wrought,
This worthy London prentice
   Was from the prison brought,
And to the lions given
   To stanch their hunger great,
Which had not eat in ten days space
   Not one small bit of meat.

But god, that knows all secrets,
   The matter so contriv'd,   90
That by this young mans valour
   They were of life depriv'd;
For, being faint for food,
   They scarcely could withstand
The noble force, and fortitude,
   And courage of his hand:

For when the hungry lions
   Had cast on him their eyes,
The elements did thunder
   With the echo of their cries: 100
And running all amain
   His body to devour,
Into their throats he thrust his arms,
   With all his might and power:

From thence, by manly valour,
   Their hearts he tore in sunder,
And at the king he threw them,
   To all the peoples wonder.

This have I done, quoth he,
  For lovely Englands sake,   110
And for my countrys maiden queen
  Much more will undertake.

But when the king perceived
  His wrathful lions hearts,
Afflictĕd with great terror,
  His rigour soon reverts;
And turned all his hate
  Into remorse and love,
And said, It is some angel,
  Sent down from heaven above.   120

No, no, I am no angel,
  The courteous young man said,
But born in famous England,
  Where gods word is obey'd;
Assisted by the heavens,
  Who did me thus befriend,
Or else they had, most cruelly,
  Brought here my life to end.

The king, in heart amazed,
  Lift up his eyes to heaven,   130
And, for his foul offences,
  Did crave to be forgiven;
Believing that no land
  Like England may be seen,
No people better governed,
  By virtue of a queen.

So taking up this young man,
  He pardon'd him his life,
And gave his daughter to him,
  To be his wedded wife.   140
Where then they did remain,
  And live in quiet peace,
In spending of their happy days
  In joy and loves increase.

XLI.

SIR ANDREW BARTON.

The story of this ballad is to be found in most of the English chronicles, under the year 1511. But the ballad, in all probability, is nearly a century more modern.

WHEN Flora, with her fragrant flowers,
  Bedeck'd the earth so trim and gay,
And Neptune, with his dainty showers,
  Came to present the month of May,
King Henry would a progress ride,
  Over the river of Thames pass'd he,
Unto a mountain top also
  Did walk some pleasure for to see;
Where forty merchants he espied,
  With fifty sail come towards him,   10
Who then no sooner were arriv'd,
  But on their knees did thus complain:

"An't please your grace, we cannot sail
  To France a voyage to be sure,
But sir Andrew Barton makes us quail,
  And robs us of our merchant-ware."

Vex'd was the king, and turning him,
  Said to his lords of high degree,
Have I ne'er a lord within my realm,
  Dare fetch that traitor unto me? 20
To him replied lord Charles Howàrd,
  I will, my liege with heart and hand,
If it please you grant me leave, he said,
  I will perform what you command.

To him then spake king Henry,
  I fear, my lord, you are too young.
No whit at all, my liege, quoth he,
  I hope to prove in valour strong.
The Scotish knight I vow to seek,
  In what place soe'er he be, 30
And bring ashore with all his might,
  Or into Scotland he shall carry me.

A hundred men, the king then said,
  Out of my realm shall chosen be;
Besides sailors and ship-boys,
  To guide a great ship on the sea;
Bow-men and gunners of good skill,
  Shall for this service chosen be;
And they, at thy command and will,
  In all affairs shall wait on thee. 40

Lord Howard call'd a gunner then,
    Who was the best in all the realm,
His age was threescore years and ten,
    And Peter Simon was his name:
My lord call'd then a bow-man rare,
    Whose active hands had gained fame,
A gentleman born in Yorkshire,
    And William Horsely was his name.

Horsely, quoth he, I must to sea,
    To seek a traitor with good speed,   50
Of a hundred bow-men brave, quoth he,
    I have chosen thee to be the head.
" If you, my lord, have chosen me
    Of a hundred men to be the head,
Upon the main-mast I'll hanged be,
    If twelvescore I miss one shillings breadth."

Lord Howard then, of courage bold,
    Went to the sea with pleasant chear,
Not curb'd with winters piercing cold,
    Though 'twas the stormy time of year.   60
Not long he had been on the sea,
    No more in days than number three,
But one Henry Hunt there he espied,
    A merchant of Newcastle was he.

To him Lord Howard call'd out amain,
    And strictly charged him to stand,
Demanding then from whence he came,
    Or where he did intend to land.

The merchant then made answer soon,
    With heavy heart, and careful mind,   70
My lord, my ship it doth belong
    Unto Newcastle upon Tine.

Can'st thou show me, the lord did say,
    As thou did'st sail by day and night,
A Scotish rover on the sea,
    His name is Andrew Barton, knight?
At this the merchant sigh'd and said,
    With grieved mind and well-away,
But over-well I know that knight,
    I was his prisoner yesterday.   80

As I, my lord, did sail from France,
    A Bourdeaux voyage to take so far,
I met with sir Andrew Barton thence,
    Who robb'd me of my merchant-ware;
And mickle debts, god knows, I owe,
    And every man doth crave his own,
And I am bound to London now;
    Of our gracious king to beg a boon.

Show me him, said lord Howard then,
    Let me but once the villain see,   90
And every penny he hath from thee ta'en,
    I'll double the same with shillings three.
Now god forbid, the merchant said,
    I fear your aim that you will miss;
God bless you from his tyranny,
    For little you think what man he is.

He is brass within, and steel without,
    His ship most huge, and mighty strong,
With eighteen pieces of ordnànce,
    He carrieth on each side along: 100
With beams for his top-castle,
    As being also huge and high,
That neither Englìsh nor Portugàl
    Can sir Andrèw Bartòn pass by.

Hard news thou show'st, then said the lord,
    To welcome strangers to the sea;
But, as I said, I'll bring him aboard,
    Or into Scotlànd he shall carry me,
The merchant said, If you will do so,
    Take counsel then I pray withall,   110
Let no man to his top-castle go,
    Nor strive to let his beams down fall.

Lend me seven pieces of ordnance then,
    On each side of my ship, quoth he,
And to-morrow, my lord, 'twixt six and seven
    Again I will your honour see:
A glass I'll set, that may be seen,
    Whether you sail by day or night,
And to-morrow, be sure, before seven,
    You shall see sir Andrew Barton, knight.   120

The merchant set my lord a glass,
    So well apparent in his sight,
That on the morrow, as his promise was,
    He saw sir Andrew Barton, knight.

The lord then swore a mighty oath,
   Now by the heavens that be of might,
By faith, believe me, and by troth,
   I think he is a worthy knight.

Fetch me my Lion out of hand,
   Saith the lord, with rose and streamer high,   130
Set up withall a willow wand,
   That merchant-like I may pass by.
Thus bravely did lord Howard pass,
   And did on anchor rise so high;
No top-sail at all he cast,
   But as a foe he did him defy.

Sir Andrew Barton seeing him
   Thus scornfully to pass by,
As though he cared not a pin
   For him and all his company;   140
Then call'd he for his men amain,
   Fetch back yon pedler now, quoth he,
And, ere this way he come again,
   I'll teach him well his courtesy.

A piece of ordnance soon was shot,
   By this proud pirate fiercely then,
Into lord Howards middle deck,
   Which cruel shot kill'd fourteen men,
He call'd then Peter Simon, he,
   Look 'now' thy word do stand in stead,   150
For thou shalt be hanged on main mast,
   If thou miss twelve-score one penny breadth.

Then Peter Simon gave a shot,
    Which did sir Andrew mickle scare,
In at his deck it came so hot,
    Kill'd fifteen of his men of war:
Alas, then said the pirate stout,
    I am in danger now I see;
This is some lord, I greatly doubt,
    That is set on to conquer me.   160

Then Henry Hunt, with rigour hot,
    Came bravely on the other side,
Who likewise shot in at his deck,
    And kill'd fifty of his men beside:
Then, Out alas! sir Andrew cried,
    What may a man now think or say?
Yon merchant thief that pierceth me,
    He was my prisoner yesterday.

Then did he on Gordion call,
    Unto the top-castle for to go,   170
And bid his beams he should let fall,
    For he greatly fear'd an overthrow.
The lord call'd Horsely then in haste,
    Look that thy word now stand in stead,
For thou shall be hanged on main-mast,
    If thou miss twelve-score a shilling breadth.

Then up the mast-tree swerved he,
    This stout and mighty Gordion;
But Horsely he, most happily,
    Shot him under his collar-bone.   180

Then call'd he on his nephew then,
   Said, Sisters sons I have no mo;
Three hundred pound I will give to thee,
   If thou wilt to the top-castle go.

Then stoutly he began to climb,
   From off the mast scorn'd to depart;
But Horsely soon prevented him,
   And deadly pierc'd him to the heart.
His men being slain, then up amain
   Did this proud pirate climb with speed,   190
For armour of proof he had put on,
   And did not dint of arrows dread.

Come hither Horsely, said the lord,
   See thou thine arrows aim aright:
Great means to thee I will afford,
   And if thou speed I'll make thee knight.
Sir Andrew did climb up the tree,
   With right good will, and all his main,
Then upon the breast hit Horsely he,
   Till the arrow did return again.   200

Then Horsely 'spied a private place,
   With a perfect eye, in a secret part;
His arrow swiftly flew apace,
   And smote sir Andrew to the heart.
" Fight on, fight on, my merry men all,
   A little I am hurt, yet not slain.
I'll but lie down, and bleed a while,
   And come and fight with you again."

And do not, said he, fear English rogues,
    And of our foes stand not in awe,   210
But stand fast by Saint Andrews cross,
    Until you hear my whistle blow.—
They never heard his whistle blow,
    Which made them all full sore afraid,
Then Horsely said, My lord, aboard,
    For now sir Andrew Barton's dead.

Thus boarded they this gallant ship,
    With right good will, and all their main,
Eighteen score Scots alive in it,
    Besides as many more were slain.   220
The lord went where sir Andrew lay,
    And quickly then cut off his head:
" I should forsake England many a day,
    If thou wert alive as thou art dead."

Thus from the wars lord Howard came,
    With mickle joy and triumphing,
The pirates head he brought along,
    For to present unto the king:
Who briefly then to him did say,
    Before he knew well what was done,   230
Where is the knight and pirate gay?
    That I myself may give the doom.

You may thank god, then said the lord,
    And four men in the ship, quoth he,
That we are safely come ashore,
    Sith you never had such an enemy;

That is, Henry Hunt, and Peter Simon,
   William Horsely, and Peters son;
Therefore reward them for their pains,
   For they did service in their turn.   240

To the merchant then the king did say,
   In lieu of what he hath from thee ta'en,
I 'll give to thee a noble a day,
   Sir Andrews whistle, and his chain:
To Peter Simon a crown a day;
   And half a crown to Peters son;
And that was for a shot so gay,
   Which bravely brought sir Andrew down.

Horsely I will make thee a knight,
   And in Yorkshire thou shalt dwell;   250
Lord Howard shall [be] earl Bury hight,
   For this title he deserveth well:
Seven shillings to our English men,
   Who in this fight did stoutly stand;
And twelve pence a day to the Scots, till they
   Come to my brother kings high land.

XLII.

JOHN ARMSTRONGS LAST GOOD-NIGHT.

Is there never a man in all Scotlànd,
    From the highest estate to the lowest degree,
That can show himself now before the king,
    Scotlànd is so full of treachery?

Yes, there is a man in Westmorelànd,
    And John Armstrong they do him call,
He has no lands nor rents coming in,
    Yet he keeps eight score men within his hall.

He has horses and harness for them all,
    And goodly steeds that be milk-white,   10
With their goodly belts about their necks,
    With hats and feathers all alike.

The king he writes a loving lettèr,
    And with his own hand so tenderly,
And hath sent it unto John Armstròng,
    To come and speak with him speedily.

When John he look'd this letter upon,
    Good lord, he 'was' as blithe as a bird in a tree:
" I was never before a king in my life,
    My father, my grandfather, nor none of us three. 20

[*V.* 18. look'd.]

But seeing we must go before the king,
  Lord we will go most gallantly;
Ye shall every one have a velvet coat,
  Laid down with golden laces three:

And you shall every one have a scarlet cloak,
  Laid down with silver laces five;
With your golden belts about your necks,
  With hats and feathers all alike."

But when John he went from Giltnock hall,
  The wind it blew hard, and full fast it did rain: 30
" Now fare thee well, thou Giltnock-hall,
  I fear I shall never see thee again."

Now John is to Edinburgh gone,
  With his eight score men so gallantly,
And every one of them on a milk-white steed,
  With their bucklers and swords hanging to their knee.

But when John came the king before,
  With his eight score men so gallant to see,
The king he mov'd his bonnet to him,
  He thought he had been a king as well as he.   40

O pardon, pardon, my sovereign liege,
  Pardon for my eight score men and me;
For my name it is John Armstròng,
  And a subject of yours, my liege, said he.

"Away with thee, thou false traitòr,
   No pardon will I grant to thee,
But, to-morrow 'morn' by eight of the clock,
   I will hang up thy eight score men and thee."

Then John look'd over his left shouldèr,
   And to his merry men thus said he,   50
I have asked grace of a graceless face,
   No pardon there is for you or me.

Then John pull'd out his nut-brown sword,
   And it was made of metal so free,
Had not the king mov'd his foot as he did,
   John had taken his head from his fair body.

"Come, follow me, my merry men all,
   We will scorn one foot for to fly,
It shall ne'er be said we were hung like dogs,
   We will fight it out most manfully."   60

Then they fought on like champions bold,
   For their hearts were sturdy, stout and free,
Till they had kill'd all the kings good guard,
   There was none left alive but two or three.

But then rose up all Edinburgh,
   They rose up by thousands three,
Then a cowardly Scot came John behind,
   And run him through the fair body.

[*V.* 47. morning.]

Said John, "Fight on my merry men all,
    I am a little wounded, but am not slain;   70
I will lay me down for to bleed a while,
    Then I'll rise and fight with you again."

Then they fought on like madmen all,
    Till many a man lay dead on the plain,
For they were resolved, before they would yield,
    That every man would there be slain.

So there they fought courageously,
    Till most of them lay dead there and slain;
But little Musgrave that was his foot-page,
    With his bonny Grissel got away unta'en.   80

But when he came to Giltnock-hall,
    The lady spied him presently:
"What news, what news, thou little foot-page,
    What news from thy master, and his company?"

My news is bad, ladỳ, he said,
    Which I do bring as you may see;
My master John Armstròng he is slain,
    And all his gallant company.

"Yet thou art welcome home, my bonny Grissèl,
    Full oft thou hast been fed with corn and hay,   90
But now thou shalt be fed with bread and wine,
    And thy sides shall be spurr'd no more, I say."

[*V.* 74. upon.]

O then bespake his little son,
  As he sat on his nurses knee,
If ever I live to be a man,
  My fathers death reveng'd shall be *."

XLIII

THE HUNTING IN CHEVY-CHASE.

Apparently modernised from a very ancient piece upon the same subject, preserved by Hearne (G. Neubri. I. lxxxii.); and now added to the present collection. An admirable Latin version, written at the command of Compton, bishop of London, by Henry Bold, is inserted among his Latin songs, and in Drydens " Collection of miscellaneous poems."

God prosper long our noble king,
  Our lives and safeties all;
A woeful hunting once there did
  In Chevy-chase befall:

To drive the deer with hound and horn,
  Earl Percy took his way;
The child may rue that is unborn
  The hunting of that day.

---

* The best account of Armstrong, his conduct, capture and execution,—for, alas! instead of ending his life so gallantly as he is here made to do, he was ignobly hanged upon a gallows,—is to be found in Lindsay of Pitscotties *History of Scotland*. (Edin. 1727, fo.) He is likewise noticed by Buchanan.—See both and other passages, in a note to a different ballad upon the same subject. *Scotish songs*, 1794, volume ii. p. 7.

The stout earl of Northumberland
   A vow to god did make,   10
His pleasure in the Scotish woods
   Three summers days to take;

The chiefest harts in Chevy-chase
   To kill and bear away:
These tidings to earl Douglas came,
   In Scotland where he lay;

Who sent earl Percy present word
   He would prevent his sport:
The English earl, not fearing this,
   Did to the woods resort,   20

With fifteen hundred bowmen bold;
   All chosen men of might,
Who knew full well, in time of need,
   To aim their shafts aright.

The gallant greyhounds swiftly ran,
   To chase the fallow deer:
On Monday they began to hunt,
   When day-light did appear;

And, long before high noon, they had
   A hundred fat bucks slain;   30
Then, having din'd, the drovers went
   To rouse them up again.

The bowmen muster'd on the hills,
    Well able to endure;
Their backsides all, with special care,
    That day were guarded sure.

The hounds ran swiftly through the woods,
    The nimble deer to take,
And with their cries the hills and dales
    An echo shrill did make.   40

Lord Percy to the quarry went,
    To view the slaughter'd deer;
Quoth he, Earl Douglas promised
    This day to meet me here:

If that I thought he would not come,
    No longer would I stay.
With that a brave young gentleman
    Thus to the earl did say:

Lo! yonder doth earl Douglas come,
    His men in armour bright;   50
Full twenty hundred Scotish spears
    All marching in our sight;

All men of pleasant Tividale,
    Fast by the river Tweed.
Then cease your sport, earl Percy said,
    And take your bows with speed:

And now with me, my countrymen,
    Your courage forth advance;
For never was there champion yet,
    In Scotland or in France,   60

That ever did on horseback come,
    But if my hap it were,
I durst encounter, man for man,
    With him to break a spear.

Earl Douglas, on a milk-white steed,
    Most like a baron bold,
Rode foremost of the company,
    Whose armour shone like gold:

Show me, said he, whose men you be,
    That hunt so boldly here;   70
That, without my consent, do chase,
    And kill my fallow-deer!

The man that first did answer make,
    Was noble Percy, he;
Who said, We list not to declare,
    Nor show whose men we be:

Yet we will spend our dearest blood,
    Thy chiefest harts to slay.
Then Douglas swore a solemn oath,
    And thus in rage did say: 80

Ere thus I will out-braved be,
  One of us two shall die:
I know thee well, an earl thou art,
  Lord Percy, so am I.

But trust me, Percy, pity it were,
  And great offence, to kill
Any of these our harmless men,
  For they have done no ill:

Let thou and I the battle try,
  And set our men aside,   90
Accurs'd be he, lord Percy said,
  By whom this is denied.'

Then stepp'd a gallant squire forth,
  Witherington was his name,
Who said, I would not have it told
  To Henry our king, for shame,

That e'er my captain fought on foot,
  And I stood looking on:
You be two earls, said Witherington,
  And I a squire alone: 100

I'll do the best that do I may,
  While I have strength to stand;
While I have power to wield my sword,
  I'll fight with heart and hand.

Our English archers bent their bows,
    Their hearts were good and true;
At the first flight of arrows sent,
    Full threescore Scots they slew.

To drive the deer with hound and horn,
    Earl Douglas had the bent;   110
A captain mov'd with mickle pride,
    The spears to shivers sent.

They clos'd full fast on every side,
    No slackness there was found;
And many a gallant gentleman
    Lay gasping on the ground.

O Christ! it was a grief to see,
    And likewise for to hear
The cries of men lying in their gore,
    And scatter'd here and there.   120

At last these two stout earls did meet,
    Like captains of great might;
Like lions mov'd, they laid on load,
    And made a cruel fight.

They fought until they both did sweat,
    With swords of temper'd steel;
Until the blood, like drops of rain,
    They trickling down did feel.

Yield thee, lord Percy, Douglas said,
   In faith I will thee bring 130
Where thou shalt high advanced be
   By James our Scotish king:

Thy ransom I will freely give,
   And thus report of thee,
Thou art the most courageous knight,
   That ever I did see.

No, Douglas, quoth earl Percy then,
   Thy proffer I do scorn;
I will not yield to any Scot
   That ever yet was born. 140

With that there came an arrow keen,
   Out of an English bow,
Which struck earl Douglas to the heart,
   A deep and deadly blow:

Who never spoke more words than these,
   Fight on, my merry men all;
For why, my life is at an end,
   Lord Percy sees my fall.

Then leaving life, earl Percy took
   The dead man by the hand, 150
And said, Earl Douglas, for thy life
   Would I had lost my land.

O Christ! my very heart doth bleed,
    With sorrow for thy sake;
For sure, a more renowned knight
    Mischance did never take.

A knight amongst the Scots there was,
    Which saw earl Douglas die,
Who straight in wrath did vow revenge
    Upon the earl Percy: 160

Sir Hugh Montgomery was he call'd;
    Who, with a spear most bright,
Well mounted on a gallant steed,
    Ran fiercely through the fight;

And pass'd the English archers all,
    Without all dread or fear;
And through earl Percys body then
    He thrust his hateful spear:

With such a vehement force and might
    He did his body gore,   170
The spear went through the other side
    A large cloth-yard, and more.

So thus did both these nobles die,
    Whose courage none could stain:
An English archer then perceiv'd
    The noble earl was slain:

> He had a bow bent in his hand,
>   Made of a trusty tree;
> An arrow of a cloth-yard long
>   Up to the head drew he: 180
>
> Against sir Hugh Montgomery
>   So right the shaft he set,
> The grey-goose-wing that was thereon
>   In his heart-blood was wet.
>
> This fight did last from break of day
>   Till setting of the sun;
> For when they rung the evening-bell*
>   The battle scarce was done.

* "That is," according to dr. Percy, "the Curfew bell, usually rung at eight o'clock." But, if this be the present authors meaning, he has deviated very widely from his original, which expressly tells us, that

> "When EVEN-SONG BELL was rang the battell was nat half done."

That it was formerly looked upon as an uncommon, and, perhaps, irreligious circumstance, for a Christian army to continue engaged after the ringing of this bell, appears from a similar passage in the ancient Catalan romance of TIRANT LO BLANCH (Barcelona, 1497, folio); where it is said, "E continuant toste'ps la batailla era ia quasi hora de vespres," &c. So, likewise, in the "Histoire du noble preux et vaillant Guerin de Montglave," (Lyon, 1585, 8vo.) "& maintint la guerre jusques à l'heure de vespres." The reason is that the angelical salutation was then sung, whence it was sometimes called The Ave-Maria bell.

With the earl Percy there was slain
    Sir John of Ogerton,
Sir Robert Ratcliffe, and sir John,
    Sir James that bold baròn:

And, with sir George, and good sir James,
    Both knights of good account,
Good sir Ralph Raby there was slain,
    Whose prowess did surmount.

For Witherington needs must I wail,
    As one in doleful dumps;
For when his legs were smitten off,
    He fought upon his stumps.

And with earl Douglas there was slain,
    Sir Hugh Montgomery;
Sir Charles Cürrèl, that from the field
    One foot would never fly;

Sir Charles Murrèl of Ratcliffe too,
    His sisters son was he;
Sir David Lamb, so well esteem'd,
    Yet saved could not be.

And the lord Maxwell, in like wise,
    Did with earl Douglas die:
Of twenty hundred Scotish spears,
    Scarce fifty five did fly.

Of fifteen hundred Englishmen,
    Went home but fifty three:
The rest were slain in Chevy-chase,
    Under the green wood tree.

Next day did many widows come,
    Their husbands to bewail;
They wash'd their wounds in brinish tears,
    But all would not prevail.   220

Their bodies, bath'd in purple blood,
    They bore with them away;
They kiss'd them dead a thousand times,
    When they were clad in clay.

This news was brought to Edinburgh,
    Where Scotlands king did reign,
That brave earl Douglas suddenly
    Was with an arrow slain.

O heavy news, king James did say,
    Scotland can witness be,   230
I have not any captain more
    Of such account as he.

Like tidings to king Henry came,
    Within as short a space,
That Percy of Northumberland
    Was slain in Chevy-chase.

Now god be with him, said our king,
   Sith 'twill no better be;
I trust I have within my realm,
   Five hundred as good as he.   240

Yet shall not Scot nor Scotland say,
   But I will vengeance take;
And be revenged on them all,
   For brave lord Percys sake.

This vow full well the king perform'd,
   After, on Humbledown;
In one day, fifty knights were slain,
   With lords of great renown;

And of the rest, of small account,
   Did many hundreds die.   250
Thus ended the hunting of Chevy-chase,
   Made by the earl Percy.

God save the king, and bless the land
   In plenty, joy, and peace;
And grant, henceforth, that foul debate
   'Twixt noblemen may cease.

Ancient Songs and Ballads.

CLASS V.

COMPRISING

THE REIGNS OF JAMES I., CHARLES I., CHARLES II.,
AND JAMES II.

I.

A LOVE SONG.

BY MASTER WITHER.

—Is given from a small miscellany in 12mo. intitled, "A description of love: with certain epigrams, elegies, and sonnets. And also Johnsons answere to master Withers. The second edition, with the crie of Ludgate, and the song of the Begger." Lond. 1620[*].—The third verse is quoted by Hearne in his notes and spicilege on William of Newborough, (p. 756.) and by him attributed to the above writer. In some editions of that humourous trifle, "The Companion to the Guide," one of the juvenile productions of the present laureat, may be found a similar song, which the ingenious author ascribes to Taylor the Water-Poet, and supposes to be older than this of Withers, being printed in 1618; a circumstance by no means conclusive; and whoever examines and compares the two pieces can scarcely hesitate a moment in deciding in favour of the following ballad, both as to antiquity and merit. To cut the matter short, however, we shall attempt to ascertain the very year in which it was written. The author was admitted of Magdalen College, Oxford, in 1604, and having pursued his studies for three years, left the University for the Inns of Chancery. Now it will be evident that this song was written at college, as well from its being clearly a youthful composition, as from the mention he makes in it of his summer excursions to Medley, "a large house between Godstow and Oxford, very pleasantly situated just by the river, and a famous place for recreation in summer time[†]." See also V. 60. If therefore we allow the first year for his falling in love, the second for the favourable return he experienced, and the third for the loss of his mistress, this song must have been written in 1606, when the author was 18 years of age. John Taylor was on all occasions the professed

---

[*] The 8th edition of this popular little book appeared in 1636, and the ninth in 1638.
[†] Hearne *ubi supra*. p. 755, 756.

antagonist of Wither, and there cannot be a doubt that the song printed by Mr. Warton is a direct parody of the following.

George Wither was born in 1588, and died in 1667. The reader will find some account of him in Percys *Reliques*, Vol. III. p. 190. and a very long one in Woods *Athenæ Oxonienses*, Vol. II. p. 391.

    I LOV'D a lasse, a faire one,
        As faire as ' e'er ' was seene;
    She was, indeed, a rare one,
        Another Sheba queene;
    But, foole, as then I was,
        I thought she lov'd me too;
    But, now, alas! sh'as left me,
        Falero, lero, loo.

    Her haire, like gold, did glister,
        Each eye was [like] a starre;   10
    Shee did surpasse her sister,
        Which past all others farre:
    Shee would me hony call,
        She'd, o she'd kisse me too!
    But, now, alasse! sh'as left me,
        Falero, lero, loo.

    In summer-time, to Medley
        My love and I would goe,
    The boat-men there stood readie,
        My love and I to rowe;   20
    For creame there would we call,
        For cakes, and for prunes too,
    But, now, alasse! sh'as left me,
        Falero, lero, loo.

Many a merry meeting
   My love and I have had;
She was my onely sweeting,
   She made my heart full glad:
The teares stood in her eyes,
   Like to the morning-dew;   30
But, now, alasse! sh'as left me,
   Falero, lero, loo.

And, as abroad we walked,
   As lovers fashion is,
Oft, as we sweetly talked,
   The sun would steale a kisse,
The winde upon her lips
   Likewise most sweetly blew;
But, now, alasse! sh'as left me,
   Falero, lero, loo.   40

Her cheekes were like the cherrie,
   Her skin as white as snow;
When she was blyth and merrie,
   She angel-like did show:
Her wast exceeding small,
   The fives did fit her shoo*:
But, now, alasse! sh'as left me,
   Falero, lero, loo.

---

* This is understood to mean, that her shoes were made upon the last *No.* 5, being one of the *smallest* size.

In summer-time or winter,
   She had her hearts desire,   50
I stil did scorne to stint her
   From sugar, sacke or fire:
The world went round about,
   No cares we ever knew;
But, now, alasse! sh'as left me,
     Falero, lere, loo.

As we walk'd home together,
   At midnight, through the towne,
To keepe away the weather,
   O're her I'd cast my gowne;   60
No colde my love should feele,
   ' Whate'er ' the heavens could doe,
But, now, alasse! sh'as left me,
     Falero, lero, loo.

Like doves we would be billing,
   And clip and kisse so fast,
Yet she would be unwilling,
   That I should kisse the last;
They're Judas kisses now,
   Since that they prov'd untrue,   70
For, now, alasse! sh'as left me,
     Falero, lero, loo.

To maidens vowes and swearing
   Henceforth nocred it give;
You may give them the hearing,
   But never them beleeve:

They are as false as faire,
   Unconstant, fraile, untrue;
For mine, alasse! hath left me,
     Falero, lero, loo.

'Twas I that paid for all things,
   'Twas ' others ' dranke the wine;
I cannot now recall things,
   Live but a foole to pine:
'Twas I that beat the bush,
   The bird to others flew;
For she, alasse! hath left me,
     Falero, lero, loo.

If ever that dame Nature,
   For this false lovers sake,
Another pleasing creature,
   Like unto her would make,
Let her remember this,
   To make the other true,
For this, alasse! hath left me,
     Falero, lero, loo.

No riches, now, can raise me,
   No want make me despaire,
No miserie amaze me,
   Nor yet for want I care:
I have lost a world it selfe,
   My earthly heaven, adue!
Since she, alasse! hath left me,
     Falero, lero, loo.

II.

A CAROL FOR PRESENTING THE WASSEL-BOWL, TO BE SUNG UPON TWELFTH-DAY AT NIGHT.

From a collection intitled, " New Christmas Carrols: Being fit also to be sung at Easter, Whitsontide, and other Festival days in the year." no date. 12mo. black letter; in the curious study of that ever to be respected antiquary Anthony à Wood, in the Ashmolean Museum.

" There was an ancient custom," says Brand, " (I know not whether it be not yet retained in many places): Young women went about with a WASSAIL-BOWL, that is, a bowl of spiced ale, on new year's eve, with some sort of verses that were sung by them in going about from door to door.... They accepted little presents from the houses they stopped at. Mr. Selden thus alludes to it in his Table Talk, Art. Pope. ' The Pope in sending relicks to princes does as WENCHES do by their WASSELS at NEW YEARS TIDE. They present you with a CUP, and you must DRINK of a SLABBY STUFF; but the meaning is, you must GIVE them MONEY, ten times more than it is worth.' " *Observations on Popular Antiquities*, p. 195. See also, p. 408. and the " Dissertation " prefixed to this collection.

Ben Jonson, in " Christmas his masque," presented at court 1616, introduces " CAROL, in a long tawney coat, with a red cap, and a flute at his girdle; his torch-bearer carrying a song-book open:" and " WASSEL, like a neat sempster and songster; her page bearing a brown bowl, drest with ribbands and rosemary before her."

   A JOLLY wassel-bowl,
    A wassel of good ale,
   Well fare the butlers soul,
    That setteth this to sale:
     Our jolly wassel!

Good dame, here, at your door,
  Our wassel we begin;
We are all maidens poor,
  We pray now let us in,
    With our wassel.

Our wassel we do fill
  With apples and with spice,
Then grant us your good will
  To tast here once or twice,
    Of our wassel.

If any maidens be
  Here dwelling in this house,
They kindly will agree
  To take a full carouse
    Of our wassel.

But here they let us stand,
  All freezing in the cold:
Good master, give command
  To enter and be bold,
    With our wassel.

Much joy into this hall
  With us is enter'd in;
Our master, first of all,
  We hope will now begin,
    Of our wassel:

And after his good wife
  Our spiced bowl will try;
The lord prolong your life!
  Good fortune we espy
    For our wassel.

Some bounty from your hands,
  Our wassel to maintain,
We'l buy no house nor lands
  With that which we do gain
    With our wassel.

This is our merry night
  Of choosing king and queen;
Then, be it your delight,
  That something may be seen
    In our wassel.

It is a noble part
  To bear a liberal mind,
God bless our masters heart!
  For here we comfort find,
    With our wassel:

And now we must be gone,
  To seek out more good cheer;
Where bounty will be shown,
  As we have found it here,
    With our wassel.

Much joy betide them all,
   Our prayers shall be still,
We hope and ever shall
   For this your great good will
      To our wassel.

III.

A CHRISTMAS CAROL.

God bless the master of this house,
   The mistress, also,
And all the little children,
   That round the table go:

And all your kin and kinsfolk,
   That dwell both far and near;
I wish you a merry Christmas,
   And a happy new year.

IV.

THE TAMING OF A SHREW.

From one of the Sloan MSS. in the Museum (No. 1489). The writing of Charles the 1sts time.

AL you that are assembled heere,
   Come listen to my song,
But first a pardon I must crave,
   For feare of further wrong;
I must entreat thes good wyves al
   They wil not angrye be,
And I will sing a merrye song,
   If they thereto agree.

Because the song I mean to sing
   Doth touch them most of all,   10
And loth I were that any one
   With me shold chide and brawle;
I have anough of that at home,
   At boarde, and eake in bed,
And once for singing this same song
   My wyfe did breake my head.

But if thes good wyves all be pleasd,
   And pleased be the men,
Ile venture one more broken pate,
   To sing it once agayne;   20

But first Ile tell you what its cald,
    For feare you heare no more,
Tis calde the Taming of a Shrew,
    Not often sung before.

And if I then shall sing the rest,
    A signe I needs must have,
Hold but your finger up to me,
    Or hem, thats al I crave;
Then wil I sing it with a harte,
    And to it roundelye goe,   30
You know my mynde, now let me see
    Whether I shal sing't or no.   *Hem.*

Well then I see you willing are
    That I shall sing the reste,
To pleasure all thes good wyves heire
    I meane to do my best,
For I doe see even by their lookes
    No hurte to me they thinke,
And thus it chancte upon a tyme
    (But first give me a drinke).   40

Not long agoe a lustye lad
    Did woe a livelye lasse,
And long it was before he cold
    His purpose bring to passe;
Yet at the lenth it thus fell out
    She granted his petition,
That she wold be his wedded wyfe,
    But yet on this condicion,

That she shold weare the breeches on
    For one yeare and a day,   50
And not to be controld of him
    Whatsoere 'she'd do, or say,'
She rulde, shee raignd, she had hir wil,
    Even as she wold require,
But marke what fell out afterwards,
    Good wyves I you desyre.

She made him weary of his lyfe,
    He wishte that death wold come,
And end his myserye at once,
    Ere that the yeare was run;   60
He thought it was the longest yeare,
    That was since he was borne,
But he cold not the matter mend
    For he was thereto sworne.

Yet hath the longest day his date,
    For this we al do know,
Although the day be neer soe long
    To even soone wil it goe;
So fell it out with hir at lenth,
    The yeare was now come out,   70
The sun, and moone, and all the starres,
    Their race had run about.

Then he began to rouse himselfe,
    And to his wyfe he saide,
Since that your raigne is at an end,
    Now know me for your heade;

        [*V.* 52. she did or said.]

But she that had borne swaye so long
  Wold not be under brought,
But stil hir tounge on pattens ran
  Though many blowes she caught.   80

He bet hir backe, he bet hir syde,
  He bet hir blacke and blew,
But for all this she wold not mend,
  But worse and worse she grew;
When that he saw she wolde not mend,
  Another way wrought hee,
He mewde hir up as men mew hawkes
  Where 'noe' light she cold see.

And kept hir without meate or drinke
  For four dayes space and more,   90
Yet for all this she was as ill
  As ere she was before;
When that he saw she wold not mend,
  Nor that she wold be quiet,
Neither for stroakes, nor locking up,
  Nor yet for want of dyet,

He was almost at his wits end,
  He knew not what to doe,
So that with gentlenes againe
  He gane his wyfe to woo;   100
But she soone bad him holde his peace,
  And sware it was his best,
But then he thought him of a wyle,
  Which made him be at rest.

[*V.* 88. loe. MS.]

He told a frend, or two of his
    What he had in his mynde,
Who went with him into his house
    And when they all had dynde;
Good wyfe (quoth he) thes frends of myne,
    Come hither for your good,   110
There lyes a vayne under your toung,
    Must now be letten blood.

Then she began to use hir tearmes,
    And rayled at them fast,
Yet bounde they hir for al hir strenth
    Unto a poast at laste,
And let hir blood under the toung,
    And tho she bled full sore,
Yet did she rayle at them as fast,
    As ere she raylde before.   120

Wel then (quoth he) the faulte I see,
    She hath it from hir mother,
It is hir teeth infects hir toung,
    And it can be noe other;
And since I now doe know the cause,
    Whatsoever to me befall,
Ile plucke hir teeth out of hir toung,
    Perhaps hir toung and all.

And with a payre of pinsers strong,
    He pluckt a great tooth out,   130
And for to plucke another thence,
    He quicklye went about,

But then she held up both her hands,
   And did for mercye pray,
Protesting that against his will
   She wold not doe nor saye.

Whereat hir husband was right glad,
   That she had changde her mynde,
For from that tyme unto hir death
   She proved both good and kynde;   140
Then did he take hir from the poast,
   And did unbynde hir then;
I wold al shrews were served thus,
   Al good wyves say Amen.

V.

TOM OF BEDLAM.

It has been already observed, "that the English have more songs and ballads on the subject of madness than any of their neighbours." Dr. Percy, whose observation this is, out of a much larger quantity, has selected half a dozen. (See *Reliques*, vol. ii. p. 350.) This and the following appear to have been written by way of burlesque on such sort of things. They are both given from an old miscellany, intitled "Le Prince d'amour, or the prince of Love. With a collection of songs by the wits of the age." London, 1660, 8vo. The tune of these songs is preserved in Durfeys "Pills to purge melancholy," iv. 189.

FROM the hag and hungry goblin,
   That into rags would rend you,
     And the spirits that stand
     By the naked man,
   In the book of moons defend you:

That of your five sound senses
   You never be forsaken,
      Nor travel from
      Yourselves with Tom
   Abroad to beg your bacon.   10
While I do sing, any food, any feeding,
   Feeding, drink or cloathing;
Come dame or maid, be not afraid,
   Poor Tom will injure nothing.

'Of' thirty bare years, have I
   Twice twenty been enraged,
      And of forty, been
      Three times fifteen
   In durance soundly caged,
On the lordly lofts of Bedlam,   20
   With stubble soft and dainty,
      Brave bracelets strong,
      And whips ding-dong,
   And wholesome hunger plenty.
Yet did I sing, &c.

With a thought I took for Maudlin,
   And a cruze of cockle-pottage,
      And a thing they call
      Skies, bliss you all!
   I fell into this dotage.   30

[*V*. 15. O.]

I slept not since the conquest,
 Till then I never waked,
  Till the rogueing boy
  Of love, where I lay,
Me found and stript stark-naked.
Yet do I sing, &c.

When I short have shorn my sowce-face,
 And swigg'd my horny barrel,
  I pawn'd my skin
  In an oaken inn,   40
As a suit of gilt apparel:
The moon's my constant mistris,
 The 'lonely' owl my marrow,
  The flaming drake,
  And night-crow make
Me musick to my sorrow.
Yet do I sing, &c.

The palsie plagues these 'fingers'
 When I plague your pigs or pullen,
  Your 'culvers' take,   50
  Or matchless make
Your chantyclear or sullen:
If I want provant, with Humph[re]y*

[*V.* 43. lowly.] [*V.* 48. palsies.]

* i. e. *Duke Humphrey*, falsely supposed to have had a monument in St. Pauls church. That vulgarly called his belonging, in fact, to a sir John Beauchamp, who dyed in 1358. Vide Stows *Survay of London*, 1598.

I sup, and when benighted
    I walk in Pauls,
        With wandring souls,
And never am affrighted.
Yet do I sing, &c.

I know more than Apollo,
    For oft, when he lies sleeping,   60
        I behold the stars
        At mortal wars,
In the wounded welkin weeping;
The moon embrace her shepherd,
    And the queen of love her 'warrior;'
        While the first doth horn
        The star in the morn,
And the next the heavenly farrior.
Yet do I sing, &c.

The Jeepsie, Snap and Tedro,   70
    Are none of Toms comradoes
        The baud I scorn,
        And cut-purse sworn,
    And the roaring-boyes bravadoes.
The sober knight and gentle
    Me trace and touch and spare not,
        But those that cross
        Poor Toms 'rynoceros'
Do what the panders dare not.
Yet do I sing, &c.   80

    [*V.* 65. farrior.]   [*V.* 78. rynoross.]

With a hoste of furious fancies,
  Whereof I am commander,
    With a burning spear,
    And a horse of the ayr,
To the wilderness I wander:
With a knight of ghosts and shadows
  I summon'd am to Turny,
    Ten leagues beyond,
    The wide worlds end,
Methinks it is no journy.   90
Yet do I sing, &c.

VI.

ANOTHER TOM OF BEDLAM.

From the top of high Caucasus,
  To Pauls-wharf near the Tower,
    In no great haste
    I easily past
In less than half an hour.
The gates of old Bizantium,
  I took upon my shoulders,
    And them I bore
    Twelve leagues and more
In spight of Turks and soldiers.   10
Sigh, sing and sob, sing, sigh and be merry,
  Sighing, singing and sobbing,
    Thus naked Tom
    Away doth run,
And fears no cold nor robbing.

From monsieur Tillies army
  I took two hundred bannors,
    And brought them all
    To 'Leaden'-hall,
  In sight of all the tannors.   20
I past Parnassus-ferry,
  By the hill call'd 'Aganippé,'
    From thence, on foot,'
    Without shooe or boot,
  I past to the isle of 'Shippey.'
Sigh, sing, &c.

O'er the Pirènean valley
  'Twixt Europe and Saint-Giles[es,]
    I walkt one night,
    By sun-shine light,   30
  Which fifteen-thousand miles is:
I landed at White-chappel,
  Near to Saint-Edmonds-berry,
    From thence I stept,
    While Charon slept,
  And stole away his ferry.
Sigh, sing, &c.

One summers-day at Shrove-tide,
  I met old Januàry,
    Being malecontent,   -   40
    With him I went
  To weep o'er old Canary,

  [*V.* 19. London.]   [*V.* 22. Aganip.]
  [*V.* 25. Ship.]

The man i' th' moon*, at Pancrass
   Doth yield us excellent claret,
     Having steel'd my nose,
     I sung, *Old Rose;*
   Tush! greatness cannot carry 't.
Sigh, sing, &c.

I met the Turkish sulton
   At Dover, near Saint-Georges,   50
     His train and him
     Did to Callis swim,
   Without ships, boats or barges.
I taught the king of Egypt
   A trick to save his cattle;
     I 'le plough with dogs,
     And harrow with hogs:
   You 'd think it I do prattle.
Sigh, sing, &c.

In a boat I went on dry land,   60
   From Carthage to Saint-Albons
     I sail'd to Spain,
     And back again;
   In a vessel made of whalebones.
I met Diana hunting,

---

* The sign, that is, of " *The man in the moon.*"

With all her nymphs attending,
  In Turnball-street *,
    With voices sweet,
  That honest place commending.
Sigh, sing, &c.   70

Diogenes, the belman,
  Walkt with his lanthorn duely,
    I' th' term among
    The lawyers throng,
  To find one that ' spoke' truly.
The Sun and Moon eclipsed
  I, very friendly, parted,
    And made the Sun
    Away to run,
  For fear he should be carted.   80
Sigh, sing, &c.

Long time have I been studying,
  My brains with fancies tearing
    How I might get
    Old Pauls a hat,
  And a cross-cloth for old Charing †.
Thus to give men and women

---

* A street in the city, inhabited, formerly, by thieves and prostitutes. See Shakspeares 2d part of K. Hen. IV. act iii. scene 2. Steevenses edition, 1790.

[V. 75. speaks.]

† Old Charing, i. e. the cross erected between London and Westminster, by K. Edward I. in memory of his beloved Eleanor. It was

In cloaths full satisfaction,
     These fruitless toyes,
       ' Rob' me of joyes, 90
     And ' keep' my brains in action.
Sigh, sing, &c.

VII.

NEWES.

From the collection at the end of Le Prince d' amour, 1660.

Now, gentlemen, if you will hear
   Strange news as I will tell to you,
Where e'er you go, both far and near,
   You may boldly say that this is true.

When Charing-cross was a pretty little boy,
   He was sent to Romford to sel swine;
His mother made a cheese, and he drank up the whey,
   For he never lòv'd strong beer, ale, nor wine.

When all the thieves in England died,
   That very year fel such a chance, 10
That Salisbury-plain would on horseback ride,
   And Paris-garden * carry the news to France.

demolished by order of the House of Commons in 1647, as popish and superstitious. See Percys *Reliques,* ii. 325. So that the present song must have been written before that time.
   [*V.* 90. robb'd.]   [*V.* 91. keeps.]

   * Paris-Garden was a celebrated bear garden on the Bankside, in the Borough.

When all the lawyers they did plead
   All for love, and not for gain,
Then 'twas a jovial world indeed,
   The Blue-boar of Dover fetcht apples out of Spain.

When landlords they did let their farms
   Cheap, because ' their ' tenants paid dear,
The weather-cock of Pauls turn['d] his tail to the wind,
   And tinkers they left strong ale and beer.   20

When misers all were griev'd in mind,
   Because that corn was grown so dear,
The man in the moon made Christmas-pyes,
   And bid the seven stars to eat good chear.

But, without a broker or coney-catcher
   Pauls-church-yard was never free,
Then was my lord mayor become a house-thatcher,
   Which was a wonderous sight to see.

When Bazing-stone did swim upon Thames,
   And swore all thieves to be just and true,   30
The sumnors and bailifs were honest men,
   And pease and bacon that year it snew.

When every man had a quiet wife,
   That never would once scold and chide,
Tom-tinker of Turvey, to end all strife,
   Roasted a pig in a blew-cowes hide.

[*V.* 18. his.]

VIII.

WHEN THE KING ENJOYS HIS OWN AGAIN.

BY MARTIN PARKER.

It is with particular pleasure that the editor is enabled to restore to the public the original words of the most famous and popular air ever heard of in this country. Invented to support the declining interest of the royal martyr, it served afterward, with more success, to keep up the spirits of the cavaliers, and promote the restoration of his son; an event it was employed to celebrate all over the kingdom*. At the revolution it of course became an adherent of the exiled family, whose cause it never deserted. And as a tune is said to have been a principal mean of depriving king James of the crown, this very air, upon two memorable occasions, was very near being equally instrumental in replacing it on the head of his son. It is believed to be a fact, that nothing fed the enthusiasm of the Jacobites, down almost to the present reign, in every corner of Great Britain, more than " The king shall enjoy his own again; " and even the great orator of the party, in that celebrated harangue which furnished the present laureat with the subject of one of his happiest and finest poems, was always thought to have alluded to it in his remarkable quotation from Virgil of

CARMINA TUM MELIUS CUM VENERIT IPSE CANEMUS!

The following song is given from a collection, intitled " The Loyal Garland, containing choice Songs and Sonnets of our late unhappy Revolutions." Lond. 1671. 12mo. black letter. Corrected by

---

* There was a new set of words written on this occasion, which it has not been the editors fortune to meet with: he is only able to recollect, from the performance of an old blind North-country crowder, that the concluding lines of each stanza were—

    ——Away with this curs'd rebellion!
    O the twenty-ninth of May, it was a happy day,
    When the King did enjoy his own again.

another copy in " A Collection of Loyal Songs." 1750. 8vo. The original title is " Upon defacing of Whitehall."

In the year 1711 appeared a small pamphlet, intitled " The Ballad of *The King shall enjoy his own again*: with a learned Comment thereupon, at the Request of Capt. Silk, dedicated to Jenny Man. By the Author of Tom Thumb " (i. e. Dr. Wagstaff). From this pamphlet a few notes have been extracted, which will be given at the end of the Song. This *Silk* appears to have been an officer of the City Militia, and to have given great offence by having this tune played as a march " before his heroic company, in their perambulation to the Artillery Ground."

WHAT Booker doth prognosticate
Concerning kings or kingdoms 'fate,'
I think myself to be as wise
As 'he' that gazeth on the skyes:
 My skill goes beyond
 The depth of a Pond,
Or Rivers in the greatest rain:
 Whereby I can tell
 All things will be well,
When the king enjoys his own again.   10

There's neither Swallow, Dove, nor Dade,
Can sore more high or deeper wade;
Nor 'show' a reason, from the stars,
What causeth peace or civil wars.
 The man in the moon,
 May wear out his shoo'n,
By running after Charls his wain:
 But all's to no end,
 For the times will not mend
Till the king enjoys his own again.   20

Full forty years this royal crown
Hath been his fathers and his own*;
And is there any one but he
That in the same should sharer be?
  For who better may
  The scepter sway
Than he that hath such right to reign?
  Then let's hope for a peace,
  For the wars will not cease
Till the king enjoys his own again.   30

Though for a time we see White-hall
With cobweb-hangings on the wall,
Instead of gold and silver brave,
Which, formerly, 'twas wont to have,
  With rich perfume
  In every room,
Delightful to that princely train;
  Which again shall be,
  When the time you see
That the king enjoys his own again.   40

Did Walker no predictions lack,
In Hammonds bloody almanack?

---

* This fixes the date of the song to the year 1643. The number was changed from time to time, as it suited the circumstances of the party. In the "Loyal Songs" it is *sixty*. And in a copy printed, perhaps at Edinburgh, about the year 1715, which contains several additional verses, though of inferior merit to the rest, it is *two thousand*.

Foretelling things that would ensue,
That all proves right, if lies be true;
 But why should not he
 The pillory foresee
Where in poor Toby once was ta'en?
 And, also, foreknow
 To th' gallows he must go,
When the king enjoys his own again. 50

Then [fears] avaunt! upon 'the' hill
My Hope shall cast 'her' anchor still,
 Untill I see some peaceful Dove
Bring home the Branch I dearly love;
 Then will I wait
 Till the waters abate,
Which 'now disturb' my troubled brain,
 Else never rejoyce
 Till I hear the voice
That the king enjoys his own again. 60

NOTES.

V. 1. "This *Booker* was a great Fishing-tackle maker in king Charles the Firsts time, and a very eminent proficient in that noble art and mystery, by application to which he came to have *skill in the Depth of Ponds and Rivers* *, as is here wisely observ'd.... He liv'd at the house in *Tower-street*, that is now the sign of the *Gun*, and being us'd to this sedentary diversion...he grew mighty cogitabund, from whence a frenzy seiz'd on him, and he turn'd enthusiast like one of our French prophets, and went about pro-

* *Pond* and *Rivers* are printed as proper names in all the copies.

gnosticating the downfall of the *King and Popery*, which were terms synonymous at that time of day. 'Tis true, *Cornelius a Lapide*, Anglice *Con. Stone*, has given him the title of a *Star-gazer;* but I have it from some of his contemporaries, that he was nothing of a *Conjuror*, only one of the *moderate* men of those times, who were tooth and nail for the destruction of the King and Royal Family, which put him upon that sort of speculation."

V. 11. "*Swallow*, *Dove*, and *Dade*, were as excellent at this time of day in the knowledge of the astronomical science, as either *Partridge*, *Parker*, or.. Dr. *Case* is now, and bred up to handicraft trades as all these were. The first was a *Corn-cutter* in *Gutter-lane*, who, from making a cure of Alderman *Pennington's* wife's great toe, was cry'd up for a great practitioner in physick, and from thence, as most of our modern quacks do, arriv'd at the name of a *Cunning Man*.... The Second was a *Cobler* in *White-cross-street*, who, when Sir William Waller passed by his stall in his way to attack the King's party in Cambridgeshire, told him, *The Lord would fight his battles for him;* and upon Sir William's success, was taken into the rebels pay, and made an *Almanack-maker* of. The last was a good innocent *Fiddle-string seller*,... who being told by a neighbouring teacher that their musick was in the stars, set himself at work to find out their habitations, that he might be instrument-maker to them; and having with much ado got knowledge of their place of abode, was judg'd by the Round-heads fit for their purpose, and had a pension assign'd him to make the *Stars* speak their meaning, and justify the villainie they were putting in practice."

V. 41. "*Toby Walker* (Note, I don't affirm that he was grandfather to the famous Dr. Walker, governor of Londonderry, who was kill'd at the battle of the Boyn, and happen'd to be overseer of the market at Ipswich in Suffolk, on account of giving false evidence at an assize held there) was a creature of Oliver Cromwell's, who, from a basket-maker on Dowgate-hill, on account of his sufferings, as was pretended in the cause of truth, was made colonel in the rebels army, and advanc'd afterwards to be one of the committee of safety. He was the person that at the battle of *Marston Moor*, broke into the King's head quarters, and seiz'd upon his Majesty's private papers, which afterwards were printed in order to render him odious to his subjects; and not without some reason, judg'd to be that abandon'd Regicide that sever'd the head of that Royal Martyr from his shoulders on a public stage before his own pallace gate."

V. 42. "*Hammond* the *Almanack maker*, was no manner of relation to colonel Hammond who had the King prisoner in the Isle of Wight, but one of that name, that always put down in a Chronological table when such and such a Royalist was executed, by way of reproach to them; by doing of which his *almanack* was said to be bloody. He was a butcher by trade, and for his zeal to the then prevailing party, made one of the inspectors of the victualling office.

IX.

JOHN AND JOAN;
OR,
A MAD COUPLE WELL MET.

To the tune of *The Paratour.*

From an old black letter copy in Major Pearsons collection. To this copy were subjoined the letters *M. P.* the initials, without doubt, of MARTIN PARKER, a Grub-street scribler and great Ballad monger of Charles the Firsts time.

You nine Castalian sisters
 That keep Parnassus hill,
  Come down to me,
  And let me bee
 Inspired with your skill;
That well I may demonstrate,
 A piece of household stuffe:
  You that are wed
  Mark what is sedd,
 Beware of taking snuffe.   10

A mad phantastic couple,
 A young man and a lasse,
  With their content,
  And friends consent,
 Resolv'd their times to passe
As man and wife together,
 And so they marry'd were;
  Of this mad match
  I made this catch,
 Which you may please ' to ' hear.   20
   [*V.* 20. may.]

They both had imperfections,
  Which might have caused strife
    The man would sweare
    And domineere,
  So, also, would his wife.
If John went to one alehouse,
  Joan ran into the next:
    Betwixt them both
    They made an oath,
  That neither would be vext.   30

Whatever did the goodman
  His wife would doe the like,
    If he was pleas'd,
    She was appeas'd,
  If he would kick, shee'd strike.
If queane or slut he cal'd her,
  She call'd him rogue and knave;
    If he would fight,
    Shee'd scratch and bite.
  He could no victory have.   40

If John his dog had beaten,
  Then Joan would beat her cat.
    If John, in scorne,
    His band would burn,
  Joan would have burnt her hat.
If John would break a pipkin,
  Then Joan would break a pot;
    Thus he and she
    Did both agree
  To waste all that they got.   50

If John would eate no victuals,
 Then Joan would be as crosse,
  They would not eat,
  But sav'd their meat,
 In that there was no losse.
If John were bent to feasting,
 Then Joan was of his mind;
  In right or wrong
  Both sung one song,
 As Fortune them assign'd.   60

In taverne or in alehouse
 If John and Joane did meet,
  Who 'e'er' was by
  In company
 Might tast their humors sweet:
Whatever John had cal'd for,
 Joan would not be out-dar'd,
  Those that lack'd drink
  Through want of chink,
 For them the better far'd.   70

Thus would they both sit drinking,
 As long as coine did last;
  Nay more than this,
  Ere they would misse,
 Good liquor for their taste,
John would have damm'd his doublet,
 His cloak or any thing,
  And Joan would pawne
  Her coife of lawne,
 Her bodkin or her ring.   80

If John were drunk and reeled,
  Then Joan would fall i' th' fire,
    If John fell downe
    I' th' midst o' th' towne,
  Beewraid in dirt and mire,
Joan, like a kind copartner,
  Scorn'd to stand on her feet,
    But down shee'd fall
    Before them all,
  And role about the street.   90

If John had cal'd his host knave,
  Joan cal'd her hostess wh—;
    For such-like crimes
    They, oftentimes,
  Were both thrust out of dore.
If John abus'd the constable,
  Joan would have beat the watch;
    Thus man and wife,
    In peace or strife,
  Each other sought to match.   100

But, mark, now, how it chanced:
  After a year or more,
    This couple mad
    All wasted had,
  And were grown very poore:
John could no more get liquor,
  Nor Joan could purchase drink;
    Then both the man
    And wife began
  Upon their states to thinke.   110

Thus beat with their own wepons,
　John, thus, to Joan did say,
　　　Sweet-heart, I see,
　　　We two agree,
　The cleane contràry way;
Henceforth let's doe in goodnesse,
　As we have done in ill,
　　　I'le do my best,
　　　Doe thou the rest:
　A match, quoth Joan, I will.　　　　120

So leaving those mad humors
　Which them before possest,
　　　Both man and wife
　　　Doe lead a life
　In plenty, peace and rest:
Now, John and Joan both, jointly,
　Doe set hands to the plough:
　　　Let all do soe,
　　　In weale or woe,
　And they'l do well enough.　　　　130

X.

PHILLIDA FLOUTS ME.

From " The Theatre of Compliments, or New Academy. Lond. 1689." 12mo. It is mentioned by the milkwoman in Waltons *Compleat Angler.* Lond. 1653. 8vo.—" What Song was it, I pray ? was it, Come Shepherds deck your heads: or, As at noon Dulcina rested: or, PHILLIDA FLOUTS ME?"—and is probably much older.
The answer is modern; by A. Bradley.
" Dulcina" is printed both by D'urfey and Percy. " Come Shepherds, &c." is not known.

  OH! what a plague is love!
   I cannot bear it;
  She will unconstant prove,
   I greatly fear it;
  It so torments my mind,
   That my heart faileth;
  She wavers with the wind,
   As a ship saileth:
  Please her the best I may,
  She loves still to gainsay;   10
  Alack, and well-a-day!
   Phillida flouts me.

  At the fair, th' other day,
   As she pass'd by me,
  She look'd another way,
   And would not spy me.

I woo'd her for to dine
   But could not get her;
Dick had her to the Vine,
   He might intreat her.   20
With Daniel she did dance,
On me she would not glance;
Oh thrice unhappy chance!
   Phillida flouts me.

Fair maid, be not so coy,
   Do not disdain me;
I am my mothers joy,
   Sweet, entertain me.
I shall have, when she dies,
   All things, that's fitting;   30
Her poultry and her bees,
   And her goose sitting;
A pair of mattress-beds,
A barrel full of shreds,
And yet, for all these goods,
   Phillida flouts me.

I often hear'd her say,
   That she lov'd posies;
In the last month of May
   I gave her roses;   40
Cowslips and gilly-flowers,
   And the sweet lilly,
I got to deck the bowers
   Of my dear Philly:

She did them all disdain,
And threw them back again;
Therefore, 'tis flat and plain,
    Phillida flouts me.

Thou shalt eat curds and cream
    All the year lasting,
And drink the chrystal stream,
    Pleasant in tasting;
Swigg whey until 'thou' burst,
    Eat bramble-berries,
Pye-lid and pastry-crust,
    Pears, plumbs and cherries;
Thy garments shall be thin,
Made of a weathers skin:
Yet all's not worth a pin,
    Phillida flouts me.

Which way soe'er I go,
    She still torments me;
And whatsoe'er I do,
    Nothing contents me;
I fade and pine away,
    With grief and sorrow;
I fall quite to decay,
    Like any shadow:
I shall be dead, I fear,
Within a thousand year,
And all because my dear
    Phillida flouts me.

Fair maiden, have a care,
    And in time take me;
I can have those as fair,
    If you forsake me:
There's Dol, the dairy-maid,
    Smil'd on me lately,
And wanton Winnifred
    Favours me greatly: 80
One throws milk on my cloaths,
Th' other plays with my nose;
What pretty toys are those!
    Phillida flouts me.

She has a cloth of mine,
    Wrought with blue Coventry,
Which she keeps as a sign
    Of my fidelity;
But if she frowns on me,
    She ne'er shall wear it;   90
I'll give it my maid Joan,
    And she shall tear it.
Since 't will no better be,
I'll bear it patiently;
Yet all the world may see
    Phillida flouts me.

XI.

A WORSHIPPER OF CRUELTY.

From a MS. in the Harleian library, No. 3511, written in the time of K. Charles the second.

You may use common shepherds so,
My sighs, at last, to stormes will grow,
And blow such scornes upon 'your' pride
Will blast all I have deified:
You are not faire whe[n] love you lacke,
Ingratitude makes all things blacke!

Oh! doe not, for a flocke of sheepe,
A golden shower when as you 'sleepe,'
Or for the tales 'Ambition' tells,
Forsake the house where Honour dwells!
In 'Damons' pallace you'le ne're shine
So bright as in that bower of mine.

[*V.* 8. sheepe.]   [*V.* 9. albition.]   [*V.* 11. Daman's.]

XII.

O ANTHONY, NOW, NOW, NOW.

From the collection at the end of *Le Prince d'Amour*. This appears to have been at one time a popular song. See " *The pleasant History of the gentle Craft.*"

In *The miseries of inforced marriage*, a play, by George Wilkins, 1607, one of the characters says, "Sirrah wag, this rogue was son and heir to *Antony, Now, Now*, and Blind Moon: and he must needs be a scurvy musician, that hath two *fidlers* to his fathers."

 Our king he went to Dover,
  And so he left the land,
 And so his grace came over,
  And so to Callice-sand;
 And so he went to Bullin,
  With soldiers strong enough,
 Like the valiant king of Cullin:
  O Anthony, now, now, now

 When he came to the city gate,
  Like a royal noble man,   10
 He could not abide their prate,
  But he call'd for the lady Nan;
 He swore that he would have her
  And her maiden-head, he did vow
 Their strong walls should not save her:
  O Anthony, now, now, now.

Tantarra went the trumps,
 And dub-a-dub went the guns,
The Spaniards felt their thumps,
 And cry'd, King Harry comes; 20
He batter'd their percullis,
 And made their bolts to bow,
He beat their men to 'a cullisse:'
 O Anthony, now, now, now.

King Harry laid about him
 With spear and eke with sword,
He car'd no more for a Frenchman
 Than I do now for a t——;
He burst their pallasadoes,
 And bang'd them, you know how, 30
He strapt their canvassadoes:
 O Anthony, now, now, now.

Up went the English colours,
 And all the bells did ring,
We had both crowns and dollers,
 And drank healths to our king,
And to the lady Nan of Bullin*,
 And her heavenly angels brow;

[*V.* 23. *Acculus.* Mr. Ritson was completely puzzled with this word, as utterly unintelligible. He proposed at one time reading "Arculus," and, at another, "like Hercules," and finally left a blank for it, in his manuscript, which it is therefore with becoming diffidence the present editor has ventured to supply.]

* *Our lady of Boulogne* was an image of "the Blessed Virgin," in the great church there, which the king ordered to be demolished:

The bonfires were seen to Flushin:
   O Anthony, now, now, now.   40

And then he brought her over,
   And here the queen was crown'd,
And brought, with joy, to Dover,
   And all the trumps did sound:
And so he came to 'London,'
   Whereas his grace lives now:
'Good' morrow to our noble king quoth I:
   'Good' morrow, quoth he, to thou!
And then he said to Anthony,
   O Anthony, now, now, now!   50

the image, not relishing confinement among hereticks, made its way back in an open boat, and was, when dr. Smollett saw it, "very black and very ugly, besides being cruelly mutilated." (*Travels*, i. 76.) It is pleasant enough to see how familiarly our ballad maker converts it into *Anne Boleyn*. Mr. Hawkins has fallen into a similar mistake. See his *Origin of the English Drama*.

It may be added that this same lady was the actual sovereign of the county of Boulogne, which was consecrated to her by Louis XI. in 1478; lest he or his successors should by the conquest of Artois, of which it was a member, become the vassal of an enemy or foreign power.

[*V.* 45. Ludow.]

XIII.

THE NEW COURTIER.

The tune is, *Chloris since thou art fled away, &c.*

From " The New Academy of Complements. Lond. 1671," 12mo. Compared with a black letter copy in one of Mr. Baynes's collections of Old Ballads.

Upon the Change, where merchants meet,
'Twixt Cornhill and Threadneedle-street,
Where wits of every size are hurl'd,
To treat of all things in the world,
  I saw a folded paper fall,
    And upon it
      These words were writ,
        Have at all!

Thought I, if, have at all, it be,
For ought I know, 'tis have at me;   10
And, if the consequence be true;
It may as well be, have at you:
  Then listen, pray, to what I shall
    In brief declare
      What's written there:
        Have at all!

I am a courtier, who, in sport,
Do come from the Utopian court,
To whisper softly in your ear
How high we are, and what we were;   20

To tell you all would be too much,
But, here and there,
A little touch:
Have at all!

I was, not many years ago,
In tattred trim, from top to toe,
But, now, my ruin'd robes are burn'd,
My rags are all to ribons turn'd,
My patches into pieces fall;
I cog a dye,   30
Swagger and lie;
Have at all!

Upon my Pantalonian pate
I wear a milleners estate;
But, when he duns me, at the court,
I shew him a protection for 't;
Whilst he doth to protesting fall;
And then I cry,
Dam me, you lie:
Have at all!   40

Since Venus shav'd off all my hair,
A powder'd perriwig I wear,
Which brings me in the golden girls,
Which I procure for lords and earls,
When love doth for a cooler call,
My fancy drives
At maids and wives:
Have at all!

My lodgings never are at quiet,
Another duns me for my diet, 50
I had of him in fifty-three,
Which I forget, so doth not he;
  I call him saucy fellow, sirrah,
    And draw my sword
      To run him thorough!
        Have at all!

Yet, once, a friend, that sav'd my life,
Who had a witty wanton wife,
I did, in courtesie, requite,
Made him a cuckold and a knight; 60
  Which makes him mount like tennis-ball:
    Whilst she and I
      Together cry
        Have at all!

But those citts are subtil slaves,
Most of them wits and knowing knaves;
We get their children, and they do
From us get lands and lordships too;
  And 'tis most fit, in these affairs,
    The land should go 70
      To the right heirs:
        Have at all!

A soldier I directly hate,
A cavalier once broke my pate,
With cane in hand he overcome me,
And took away my mistress from me:

For I confess, I love a wench;
　Though English, Irish,
　Dutch or French:
　　Have at all!　　　　　　　　80

A soldiers life is not like mine,
I will be plump when he shall pine;
My projects carry stronger force
Than all his armed foot and horse;
　What though his morter-pieces roar,
　　My chimney-pieces
　　Shall do more:
　　　Have at all!

Thus have I given you, in short,
A courtier of Utopia[s] court;　　　　90
I write not of religion,
For (to tell you truly) we have none.
　If any me to question call
　　With pen or sword,
　　Hab-nab's the word:
　　　Have at all!

XIV.

THE DEFEAT OF THE SPANISH ARMADA.

From "Westminster Drollery. Or, A Choice Collection of the Newest Songs and Poems, both at Court and Theatres. By a person of quality. With additions. London, 1672," 12mo. It is probably very little older than the date of the book. The tune may be found in Durfeys "Pills to purge melancholy," vol. iv. p. 32.

SOME years of late, in eighty-eight,
   As I do well remember,
It was, some say, the nineteenth of May,
   And, some say, in September,
   And, some say, in September.

The Spanish train lanch'd forth amain,
   With many a fine bravado,
Their (as they thought, but it prov'd not)
   Invincible Armado,
   Invincible Armado,   10

There was a little man, that dwelt in Spain,
   Who shot well in a gun-a,
Don Pedro hight, as black a wight
   As the Knight of the Sun-a*,
   As the Knight of the Sun-a.

* The hero of an old romance translated from the Spanish, under the title of "The Mirrour of knighthood," several volumes, 1598, &c. 4to. black letter. The person meant by don Pedro was Alonzo Perez de Guzman, duke of Medina Sidonia, commander of the Spanish fleet.

King Philip made him admiral,
    And bid him not to stay-a,
But to destroy both man and boy,
    And so to come away-a,
    And so to come away-a.   20

Their navy was well victualled,
    With bisket, pease and bacon;
They brought two ships, well fraught with whips,
    But I think they were mistaken,
    But I think they were mistaken.

Their men were young, munition strong,
    And, to do us more harm-a,
They thought it meet to join the fleet,
    All with the prince of Parma,
    All with the prince of Parma.   30

They coasted round about our land,
    And so came in by Dover;
But we had men set on 'um, then,
    And threw the rascals over,
    And threw the rascals over.

The queen was, then, at Tilbury,
    What could we more desire-a?
And sir Francis Drake, for her sweet sake,
    Did set them all on fire-a,
    Did set them all on fire-a.   40

Then, strait, they fled, by sea and land,
  That one man kill'd three score-a;
And had not they all ran away,
  In truth, he had kill'd more-a,
  In truth, he had kill'd more-a.

Then let them neither brag nor boast,
  But, if they come agen-a,
Let them take heed, they do not speed
  As they did, you know when-a.
  As they did, you know when-a. 50

XV.

THE PRODIGALS RESOLUTION;

OR,

MY FATHER WAS BORN BEFORE ME.

BY THOMAS JORDAN.

From "London Triumphant," 1672, 4to. This Jordan was the professed pageant-writer and poet-laureat for the city, and really seems to have possessed a greater share of poetical merit than usually fell to the lot of his profession. He also published "A royal arbour of loyal poesie, consisting of poems and songs." London, 1663, 12mo. (printed likewise under the title of "Musick and poetry, songs and poems, with notes"...) three or four plays, and several other small pieces.

I AM a lusty, lively, lad,
  Now come to one and twenty;
My father left me all he had,
  Both gold and silver plenty;

Now, he's in grave, I will be brave,
   The ladies shall adore me,
I'le court and kiss, what hurt's in this?
   My dad did so before me.

My father was a thrifty sir,
   Till soul and body sundred;   10
Some say, he was a usurer,
   For thirty in the hundred;
He scrapt and scratcht, she pinch'd and patch'd,
   That in her body bore me;
But I'le let flie, good reason why,
   My father was born before me.

My daddy has his duty done,
   In getting so much treasure;
I'le be as dutiful a son,
   For spending it at pleasure: 20
Five pound a quart shall chear my heart,
   Such nectar will restore me;
When ladies call, I'le have at all:
   My father was born before me.

My grandam liv'd at Washington,
   My grandsir delv'd in ditches,
The son of old John Thrashington,
   Whose lanthorn leathern-breeches
Cry'd, '*Whither*' go ye, '*whither*' go ye?
   Though men do now adore me,   30
They ne'ere did see my pedigree;
   Nor who was born before me.

My grandsir striv'd and wiv'd and thriv'd,
    Till he did riches gather,
And when he had much wealth atchiev'd,
    O, then, he got my father.
Of happy memory cry I,
    That e'ere his mother bore him,
I had not been worth one penny,
    Had I been born before him.   40

To free-school, Cambridge and Grays Inn,
    My gray-coat grandsir put him,
Till to forget he did begin
    The leathern breech that got him:
One dealt in straw, the other in law,
    The one did ditch and delve it,
My father store of satin wore,
    My grandsir beggars-velvet.

So I get wealth, what care I if
    My grandsir were a sawyer?   50
My father prov'd to be [a] chief,
    Subtle and learned lawyer:
By 'Cokes' reports and tricks in court[s],
    He did with treasure store me,
That I may say, Heavens bless the day,
    My father was born before me!

Some say, of late, a merchant, that
    Had gotten store of riches,
In 's dining-room hung up his hat,
    His staff and leathern-breeches,   60

His stockings, garter'd up with straws
   Ere providence did store him;
His son was sheriff of London, 'cause,
   His father was born before him.

So many blades that rant in silk,
   And put on scarlet cloathing,
At first did spring from butter-milk,
   Their ancestors worth nothing:
Old Adam and our grandam Eve,
   By digging and by spinning,   70
Did to all king's and princes give
   A radical beginning.

My father, to get my estate,
   Though selfish yet was slavish,
I'l[l] spend it at another rate,
   And be as lewdly lavish:
From madmen, fools and knaves he did
   Litigiously receive it,
If so he did, Justice forbid
   But I to such should leave it!   80

At playhouses and tennis-court,
   I'l[l] prove a noble fellow,
I'l[l] court my doxies to the sport
   Of, O brave Punchinello!
I'le dice and drab and drink and stab,
   No Hector shall out-roar me;
If teachers tell me tales of hell,
   My father is gone before me.

XVI.

THE HONEST FELLOW.

From " The New Academy of Compliments, 1671." Corrected by
a copy in " The Theatre of Compliments, 1689."

HANG fear, cast away care,
  The parish is bound to find us;
Thou and I, and all must die,
  And leave this world behind us.

The bells shall ring, the clerk shall sing,
  And the good old wife shall winde us;
And the sexton shall lay our bodies in the clay,
  Where nobody shall find us.

XVII.

THE BELGICK BOAR.

To the tune of *Chevy-chase*.

As this collection is brought down to and closed by the Revolution, it was thought not improper to conclude it with a relation of that celebrated event by some minstrel or ballad-maker of the time. The following Song (though not printed, it should seem, till some years after, the white letter sheet from which it is given being dated at London, 1695), has been judged as curious and interesting as any; and as it is apparently written with all the fidelity and candour with which a party matter could be well represented, will doubtless meet the readers approbation.

God prosper long our noble king,
   Our hopes and wishes all;
A fatal landing late there did,
   In Devonshire, befall.

To drive our monarch from his throne
   Prince Naso took his way:
The babe may rue that's newly born,
   The landing at Torbay.

The stubborn Tarquin, void of grace,
   A vow to hell does make,   10
To force his father abdicate,
   And then his crown to take:

And eke the royal infant prince,
   To seize or drive away.
These tidings to our sovereign came,
   In Whitehall where he lay.

Who, unconcern'd at the report,
   At first would not believe,
That any of his royal race
   Such mischiefs could conceive.   20

Till time, which ripens all things, did
   The villainy disclose;
And, of a nephew and a son,
   Forg'd out the worst of foes:

Who, by infernal instinct led,
   A mighty fleet prepares,
His fathers kingdom to invade,
   And fill his heart with cares.

Our gracious king desires to know,
   What his pretensions were,   30
And how, without his leave, he ' dar'd '
   Presume on landing here.

Declaring what was deem'd amiss,
   Should soon amended be,
And whatsoe'er should be desir'd,
   He would thereto agree:

And, for a speedy parliament,
   He doth forthwith declare;
The surly brute, not minding this,
   Does to our coast repair.   40

With several thousand Belgick boars,
   All chosen rogues for spight,
Join'd with some rebels, who, from hence
   And justice, had ta'ne flight.

Who, arm'd with malice and with hopes,
   Soon threw themselves on shoar;
Crying, religion and our laws
   They came for to restore.

Then declarations flew about
   As thick as any hail,   50
Which, though no word was ' e'er ' made good,
   Did mightily prevail.

We must be papists or be slaves,
   Was then the general cry;
But we'll do any thing to save
   Our darling liberty.

We'll all join with a foreign prince
   Against our lawful king;
For he from all our fancy'd fears
   Deliverance doth bring.   60

And if what he declares proves true,
   As who knows but it may,
Were he the devil of a prince,
   We'll rather him obey.

Then our allegiance let's cast off,
   James shall no longer guide us;
And though the French would bridle us,
   None but the Dutch shall ride us:

And those who will not join with us,
   In this design so brave,   70
Their houses we'll pull down or burn,
   And seize on what they have.

These growing evils to prevent,
    Our king his force does bend;
But, amongst those he most did trust,
    He scarce had left one friend.

O, how my very heart does bleed,
    To think how basely they
Who long had eaten royal bread,
    Their master did betray!   80

And those to whom he'd been most kind
    And greatest favours shown,
Appear'd to be the very first
    Who sought him to dethrone.

O, Compton! Langston*! and the rest
    Who basely from him ran;
Your names for ever be accurs'd
    By every English man!

Proud Tarquin, he pursues his game,
    And quickly makes it plain,   90
He came not to redress our wrongs,
    But Englands crown to gain:

---

* Lieut. Col. Langston was the first officer that deserted, with his regiment, from the kings army at Salisbury. Lieutenant-colonel sir Francis Compton, with his regiment, was of the same party, but had not the courage to go forward: it should seem, however, that he, soon afterward, made a more successful attempt.

And 'o'er' his fathers mangled fame
  His chariot proudly drives,
Whilst he, good man, although in vain,
  To pacifie him strives.

But he, ingrateful! would not hear
  His offers though so kind,
But caus'd the noble messenger*
  Forthwith to be confin'd.   100

He brings his nasty croaking crew
  Unto his fathers gate,
Dismist his own, makes them his guard:
  Oh dismal turn of fate!

And so, at midnight, drives him thence
  O horrid impious thing!
Were such affronts 'e'er' offer'd to
  A father and a king?

A king so great! so good! so just!
  So merciful to all!   110
His vertue was his only fault,
  And that which caus'd his fall:

Who now is forc'd, his life to save,
  To fly his native land,
And leave his scepter to be grasp'd
  By an ungracious hand.

          * The earl of Feversham.

Hells journey-men are streight conven'd,
    Who rob god of his power,
Set up themselves a stork-like king,
    The subjects to devour: 120

And, to secure his lawless throne,
    Now give him all we have,
And make each free-born English heart
    Become a Belgick slave.

The bar, the pulpit and the press,
    Nefariously combine,
To cry up a usurped power,
    And stamp it right divine.

Our loyalty we must melt down,
    And have it coin'd anew;   130
For, what was current heretofore,
    Will now no longer do.

Our fetters we ourselves put on,
    Ourselves ourselves do bubble;
Our conscience a meer pack-horse make,
    Which now must carry double.

O England! when to future times,
    Thy story shall be known,
How will they blush to think what crimes
    Their ancestors have done!   140

But, after all, what have we got
   By this our dear-bought king?
Why, that our scandal and reproach
   Throughout the world does ring:

That our religion, liberties,
   And laws, we held so dear,
Are more invaded since this change
   Than ever yet they were:

Our coffers drain'd, our coin impair'd
   (That little that remains);   150
Our persons seiz'd, nay thoughts arraign'd,
   Our freedom now in chains:

Our traffick ruin'd, shipping lost,
   Our traders most undone;
Our bravest heroes sacrific'd,
   Our ancient glory gone:

A fatal costly war entail'd
   On this unhappy isle;
Unless, above what we deserve,
   Kind heaven, at last, does smile;   160

And bring our injur'd monarch home,
   And place him on his throne;
And to confusion bring his foes,
   Which god grant may be soon!

Glossary.

GLOSSARY.

*** The additional explanations, for which the present editor alone is answerable, are inclosed within brackets.

A.

A. [of.]
Abatede. i. 32. ceased, did not attempt. Q.
Aboht. bought.
Abone. [above.]
Aboven. [above.]
Abugge. aby, suffer for it.
Aby. suffer for.
Acculus. ii. 274. [f. A cullisse. O. FR. strained meat.]
Adoun. [down.]
Adred. [part. pa. of aðneðe, SAX. afraid.]
Adrenche. drown, be drowned.
Af. [have.]
Aferre. afeared, afraid.
Affe. i. 47.
After. i. 40.
Agayn. [against.]
Agynneth. begin[eth.]
Ahtc. i. 67.
Alast. at last, lately.
Albydene. [altogether, wholly, entirely.]
Ald. [old.]
Alemaigne, Alemayne. [Germany.]
Algate. i. 73. [together.]
Alles. i. 30. For alles cunnes res.
Allinge. i. 30.
Als. [as.]
Amang. [among, together, at the same time. SAX.]
Amarstled. i. 70.
And. [if. SAX.]
Ane. a, [an, one.]
Angelis. [angels.]
Anonen. anon, forthwith.
Ant. and.
Apan. upon.
Aplyht. Y telle yt ou aplyht. i. 33. I tell it you rightly, perfectly, just as it was.
Aquelleden. killed.

GLOSSARY.

Aquoy. ii. 166.
Ar. [*ere, ever, before.*]
Aras. [*arrows.*]
Arewe. *rue, be vexed at.*
Arwe. [arew. *arrow.*]
Asad. Never nes *asad.* i. 28. *was never sad, never repented him.*
Ase. *as.*
Aselkethe. v. Selkethe.
Assembleden. [*assembled.*]
Assoygne. *essoign, excuse, delay.*
Ate. [*at.*]
At-ere. i. 43.
Athe. [*o' th,' of the.*]
Ather. [*either.*]
Ato. [*in two.*]
At-one. [*agreed.*]
Aught. [*ought.*]
Averil. *April.*
Avowe. [*vow.*]
Avowerie. *protection.*
Avutrie. *adultery.*
Awe. *ewe.*
Ay. [*a.*]
Ayene. Ayeyn. Ayeynes. [*again,*] *against.* Ther nis non *ayeyn* star. i. 32. *there is no opposing destiny.*
Ayens. [*for, upon.*]
Ayght. [*height.*]

B.

Bachelerys. [*bachelors.*]
Baite. i. 45.
Bald. [*bold.*]
Baldly. [*boldly.*]
Bale. *wretchedness, misery,* [*sorrow.*]
Balys. [*sorrows.*]
Bandoun. In hire *bandoun.* i. 56. *at her command.*
Bane. [*bone.*]
Baner. [*banner.*]
Bar. [*bare, bore.*]
Bare. [*bear.*]
Barn. [*child.*]
Bassonettes. [*helmets.* Bacinet. O. FR.]
Bathe. [*both.*]
Battes. i. 87.
Baylies. [*bailiffs.*]
Bayly. i. 70. [*bailiff, prison.* FR.]
Be. *been,* i. 33. [*by,* i. 87.]
Bealte. *beauty.*
Bed. [*bid.*]
Bede. [*offer; engage,* bætan, SAX.]
Beerys. [*biers.*]
Beforn. Beforne. | *before.* SAX.]
Bch. i. 61.
Beleve. [*belief.*]

Ben. [*be.*]
Bende. [*bondage, bands, bonds, prison:* benðe, Sax. *bended, bent.*]
Bene. i. 62.
Bent. [*In strictness ground near the sea, on which bent (a species of coarse grass) grows; but sometimes used for field, in a general sense: as we say the "field of battle."*]
Beo. [*be.*]
Beoth. [*be.*]
Berne. [*man, person, strictly child.* beaρn, Sax.]
Bernen. To bernen. *to be burned.*
Beseke. [*beseech.*]
Besene. i. 91.
Bete. [*heal.* "To *bete* sorwe." Chaucer.]
Betere. [*better.*]
Beth. *be.*
Bi. [*by.*]
Bide. *pray.*
Biforin. [*before.*]
Bigane. i. 41.
Bigynne. [*begin.*]
Biheveded. *beheaded.*
Bilyve. [*forthwith.*]
Binkes. [*banks.*]
Bi-northen. i. 43.

Bisette. i. 42.
Bith. *be-eth, is.*
Bityde. [*betide.*]
Blake. *black.*
Blane. [*stopped, ceased.* blınnan, Sax.]
Blenked. i. 49.
Bleo. *colour, complexion.*
Blinne. i. 49. See Blynne.
Blosme. Blosmes. Blosmen. [*blossom,*] *blossoms.*
Blowe. *breathe.*
Blykyeth. *shineth.*
Blynne. i. 28. *properly stop, cease; and hence, in this place, change, mend.*
Blysfol. [*blissful.*]
Blyve. *quickly, instantly.*
Bobaunce. *boasting.*
Bocher. *butcher.*
Bohten. *bought.*
Bollys. [*bowls.*]
Bond. [*bound.*]
Bone. i. 46. [*gone.*]
Bord. *the table.*
Boro. *pledge, surety.*
Borowed. [*redeemed.*]
Bost. [*boast.*]
Bot. Bote. [i. 23. *unless,*] i. 40. *but.*
Bote. i. 56. *better.*
Bote. [*recompence, amendment, purpose.* boτ, SAX.]

Bot-forke. *It was suggested to the editor, by an ingenious friend, that* Bot-forke *may signify the fork on which the tenant carried home his* fire-bote, *or customary allowance of wood for firing.*

Botones. [*buttons.*]

Bots. A bots. ii. 181.

Boure. *a ladys chamber.*

Bous. i. 70.

Bowen. Bowyn. Bowynd. *ready, prepared.*

Bowndyn. *bound. obliged.*

Bowne. Busk and *bowne. make ready and go.*

Bowyn. i. 95. [*went.*]

Brade. Brede. [*broad.*]

Brave. ii. 180.

Brawl. *a French dance.*

Brayd. At a *brayd. at once, on a sudden, in the instant.*

Bred. *bread.*

Brede. *breadth.* O brede and o leynthe. i. 32. *far and wide.*

Brede. i. 142.

Breme. i. 58. 64. [*sweet, clear.*]

Brennand drake. i. 89. [*says Dr. Percy, may perhaps be the same as fire-drake, or fiery serpent, a meteor or fire-work so called: Here it seems to signify burning embers, or fire brands.*]

Brenne. *burn.*

Brennynge. *burning.*

Brest. [*burst.*]

Brether. [*brethren.*]

Brid. Bridde. Bryd. *bird.*

Broche. [*a kind of buckle, broad, round, and worn on the breast, or on the hat with a tongue; a breastpin.* FR. *A brooch.*]

Brode-henne. [*brood hen.*]

Brohte. [*brought.*]

Bronde. [*A sword.* (*brand.*)]

Brok. [*brook.*]

Brook. Brouke. [*enjoy* bɲucan, SAX.]

Brotyll. *brittle.*

Brouth. [*brought.*]

Browd. i. 106. [*broad.*]

Browen. *brows.*

Brues. i. 41.

Brugge. *bridge.*

Bryk. *breeches.*

Bryttlynge. [*cutting up, quartering, carving,* Percy.]

Bue. *be.*

Buen. *been.*

Bueth. *be.*

GLOSSARY. 301

Buirdes. *birds: a term of endearment or politeness in addressing the fair sex.*

Burde. *bird, maiden, young woman.*

Burel. *coarse cloth of a brown colour.*

Burnes (or Bernes). *sirs or masters.*

Buske. [*to dress, prepare or make ready.*]

Byckarte. [*bickered, fought or skirmished.*]

Byd. *abides. suffers.*

Byddyn. *ask, invite.*

Byddys. [*abides.*]

Byde. [*abide, await.*]

Bydene. *presently, by and by.*

Byhet. *promised.*

Byleyn. i. 67.

Byn. [*be, been.*]

Byreved. " that him wes *byreved,*" i. 33. *that he was bereaved or deprived of; that was taken away from him.*

Bysoht. i. 170.

Byste. [*beest,* art.]

Byswyken. [*betrayed, beguiled, deceived.* beɼpycan, SAX.]

Bytake. i. 33.

Bythenche. *bethink.*

C.

Calve. *calf.*

Can. [*gan, began to.*]

Cannes. [*wooden or tin bowls or vessels for carrying milk or water.* canne, SAX.]

Cantelles. [*pieces, fragments.* SAX.]

Capul. [*a horse.*]

Carke. [*To feel care or anxiety.*]

Carpe. [*to talk.*]

Carpyng. *talking, speech, composition recited or repeated.*

Cas. [*case.* FR.]

Cawte. [*cautious.*]

Cawthe. i. 139.

Caym. *Cain.*

Caynard. *knave, scoundrel, &c.* [Cagnard *or* Caignard. FR.] "Sire olde *Kaynard.*" Chaucer.

Cen. [*ken. know.*]

Certyl. *kirtle, waistcoat.*

Chanoun. [*canon.* FR.]

Char. i. 67.

Chele. [*chilliness, cold.*]

Chere. [*countenance, face.*]

302 GLOSSARY.

Cherld. *churl.*
Chese. [*choose.*]
Cheventeyn. *chieftain, captain.*
Cheverone. i. 91.
Cheyn. [*chain.*]
Chil. [*child.*]
Chivauche. [*An expedition.* Chevachie. FR.]
Chose. [*to choose.*]
Chylder game. [*childs play.*]
Chylderin. (*children*) *brave men.*
Clappe. i. 51. [*Perhaps* clip, *to cut.*]
Clef. [*cleft.*]
Clepe. [*call.*]
Clepyn. *called.*
Clerk. *scholar.*
Clogs. i. 117.
Closeden. [*inclosed.*]
Cloude. *clod.*
Cokenay. [" Every fyve and fyve had a *cokenay,*" Chau.; *that is (as Mr. Tyrwhitt with great probability supposes) a cook or scullion, to attend them.*]
Collayne. [Cologne. " *Cologn steel.*" Percy.]
Compas. [*design.*]
Con. [Conne.] *can.*

Continaunce. *countenance, behaviour.*
Coroune. [*crown.*]
Cors. [i. 88. *body.* FR. i. 108. *curse.*]
Corsiare. [*courser, steed.*]
Cos. *kiss.*
Cothe. *quoth, saith.*
Couthe. *could.*
Coynte. *quaint or cunning.*
Crech. i. 93.
Crepyls. [*cripples.* SAX.]
Cressawntes. i. 101.
Crouth. *crowd, a sort of fiddle.*
Crowne. [*head.*]
Crustlik. i. 41.
Cu. *cow.*
Cuccu. *cuckow.*
Curtel. i. 36. *kirtle, a short garment; it sometimes means a waistcoat, but here, perhaps, a sort of frock.*

D.

Dabbeth. *knock*[*eth.*]
Dampned. [*condemned.*]
Dar. [*dare.*]
Dare. [For hire love y droupne ant *dare.* i. 61. '*hurt or distress myself.*' ꝺeꝵe, SAX.]
Desse. ii. 34.
Dawe. *dawn.*

Dayeseyes. *days eyes;* or, as now corruptly written, *daisies.*
De. i. 108. [*die.*]
De. Dee. *god.* dieu, FR. [Par la grace *dee*. i. 82. *by gods grace.*]
Deawes. *dews.*
Deddeth. *did.*
Dede. *death.*
Deie. [*die.*]
Del. *devil.*
Dele. [*to part, divide.*]
Delyvren. [*deliver.*]
Deme. *judge, rule, govern.*
Dent. [*stroke, blow.*]
Deores. i. 64.
Deorly. [*dearly, kindly.*]
Der. [*dear, sad, harmful, unfortunate.* ꝺeꞃe, SAX.]
Deray. [*noise. desroy,* FR.]
Dereworthe. [" SAX. *precious, valued at a high rate.*" Tyrwh.]
Dereworthliche. i. 61. [*worthily.*]
Derne. *secret.*
Destaunce. i. 52.
Deth. [*doth.*]
Deye. Dyen. [*to die.*]
Do. [*done.*]
Dogh-trogh. [*a dough-trough, a kneading trough.*]

Doh. [*do.*]
Dome. *judgement, sentence.*
Domes. i. 64.
Don. [*do.* SAX.]
Done. [*down.*]
Donketh. *moisten[eth.]*
Donnyd. [*dun.*]
Doren. i. 69. *doors.*
Doughete. ["*doughty man.*" Percy.]
Dounes. *downs.*
Doussé-pers. [FR.] *lords or barons, nobility in general, any indefinite number; originally the twelve peers of Charlemagne.*
Douteth. *feareth.*
Doys. [*does.*]
Drawe. To drawe. *to be drawn.*
Dre. [*suffer.* SAX.]
Drede. [*dread, fear, doubt.* SAX.]
Dreeg. [*drag.*]
Dreynte. *drowned.*
Drogh. Droh. [*pa. t. of* Draw. *drew.* SAX.]
Droupne. *droop.*
Drowe. [To-drowe.] *draw, drawn.*
Drue. *dry.*
Drye. [*bear, sustain, endure, suffer.* aꝺꞃeoᵹan, SAX.]

Dryng. [*drink.*]
Dude. [*did.*]
Dudest. [*didst.*]
Duere. *dear.*
Dueres. i. 66.
Dunt. *dint, stroke.*
Dur. [*dare.*]
Dutten. i. 69. *shut, fasten.*
Dwer. *fear, doubt.*
Dych. *dish.*
Dyght. Dyhte. [*dressed, decked, disposed, arranged.* SAX.]

E.

Eche. [*to add to, to encrease, eke.* SAX.]
Eghe. *eye.*
Elbouthe. [*elbow.*]
Elidelik. i. 41.
Em. [*them.*]
Eme. [*uncle.* SAX.]
Enchesoun. [*cause, occasion,*] *reason.*
Encumbre. [*encumbrance.*]
Englelonck. [*England.*]
Envye. [*hatred, malice, injury.*]
Eny. [*any.*]
Er. [*ere.*]
Ere. *heir, inherit, possess.*
Ernde. [*errand.*]
Erytage. [*heritage.*]

Es. [*is.*]
Everilk. [*every.*]
Everuche. [*every.*]
Everuchon. *every one.*

F.

Fa. i. 44. [*fast?*]
Facche. Faccheth. *fetch,* [*fetcheth.*]
Fald. i. 47. [*fell.*]
Falden. Be-falden. i. 44. [*befal.*]
Fale. [Fele.] *many.* Other *fale.* i. 74. *many other.*
Faleweth. *fadeth, grows yellow or brown, i. e. withers.*
Falle. i. 48. [*befall?*]
Fallen. [*fall.*]
Falsed. [*falsehood.*]
Falyfder. *fallow deer.*
Fande. *found.*
Fang. *See* Fenge.
Fannes. ["*instruments for winnowing corn.*" Percy.
Fare. [*to go.*]
Fare. Fare so hit *fare.* i. 54.
Faste bi. *close by.*
Faute. i. 47. [*want, fault?*]
Fay. *faith, fealty.*
Fayn. *eager, desirous.*
Fech. [*fetch.*]
Fedyrs. [*feathers.*]

GLOSSARY.

Fel. Fele. Feole. [*many*, SAX.]
Feld. i. 44. [*field. On field?*]
Felle. i. 55. *fall from?*
Felle. *skin.*
Fen. Fen of fote. i. 61.
Fen. [*mud, mire, filth.* ꝼenn, SAX.]
Fend. [*defend.*]
Fenge. [*take.* ꝼenȝan, SAX.]
Fenyl. i. 64.
Ferdnis, *fear.*
Fere. [*companion.*]
Feren. *brothers, companions.*
Ferlick. [*wonderful.*]
Ferly. [*wonder.* Ferli frained. i. 42. *wonderously asked.*]
Ferly fele. *wonderfully many, in astonishing numbers.*
Fette. [*fetched.*]
Feye. *faith.*
Ficle. *fiddle.*
Fille. i. 64.
Flagrant. [*glowing.* Johnson.]
Fleme. Ant wyht in wode be *fleme.* i. 64. *And quite into the wood be banished; and banish myself wholly into the woods.* Q. i. 78. *banish.*
Flemed. [*banished.*]
Fles. [*fleece.*]
Flesse. Fleych. *flesh, venison.*
Flo. i. 53. '*flay.*'

Flo. i. 82. *arrow.* ꝼla, SAX.
Flour. [*flower.*]
Flour de lis. [*The lily.* FR.]
Fol. [*full.*]
Foles. [*fools, vagabonds.*]
Fon. [*foen.*] *foes.*
Fond. *attempt, endeavour.*
Fonde. i. 58. v. 4. [*meet with, find?*]
Fondement. *fundamentally.*
Fong. Fonge. *take, receive.* Now ichulle *fonge* ther ich er let. i. 32. *now I will take up where I before left off.* Q.
For. [*four.*]
Fore. To fore. *before.*
Foreward. *promise, covenant.*
Forfare. *forfeit, lose, destroy.*
For-feight. [*over-fought.*]
Forgon. i. 64. [*forego?*]
Forlore. *lost, undone.*
Forsoke. [*forsake.*]
Forst. *frost.*
Forté. for to. To be pronounced as a dissyllable.
Forthi. *on this account, therefore, for this,* [*for that.* ꝼorði. SAX.]
Forthirmar. [*furthermore.*]
Forthorin. i. 49.
Forwake. *weak, strengthless.*
Foryit. [*forgot.*]
Fot. [*foot.*]

VOL. II.   X

Foul. *bird.*
Founde. To founde. i. 67.
Foursithe. *four times.*
Fowarde. [*the van.*]
Fowkin. [*See* Reliques. ii. 395. in *v.*]
Fowndyn. [*found.*]
Fra. [*from.*]
Fraine. [*ask.*]
Fray. i. 144.
Free. Freke. [man. ᚠᚱᛖᚳ, SAX.]
Frele. i. 126. *frail?*
Freoh. i. 66. [*free, noble?*]
Frere. [*friar,* FR.]
Frith. i. 50.
Fuger. *figure.*
Fullaris. *fullers.*
Fundid. i. 42.
Fur. i. 49.
Fyke. i. 67.
Fylde. i. 99. v. 109.
Fyn. *end.*

G.

Ga. Gae. [*go.*]
Gadelyngys. [*idle fellows,* SAX.]
Gadryng. [*gathering.*]
Gaf. [*gave.*]
Galewes. [*gallows.*]
Gane. [*go.*]
Gar. i. 50. [*cause?*]
Garde. i. 110. [*caused?*]
Garre. [*make.* SAX.]
Garste. i. 37.
Gates. i. 44.
Gayntyl. *gentle.*
Gedere. *gather, assemble.*
Gederede. [*gathered.*]
Gentyll. [FR. *in its original sense means well-born; of a noble family. . . It is commonly put for courteous, liberal, gentlemanlike."* Tyrwh.]
Geth. *goeth.*
Gettyng. i. 97. [*"what he had got, his plunder, booty."* Percy.]
Getyn. [*get.*]
Geynest. i. 57.
Gif. [*give.*]
Glede. [*a bright fire.*]
Go. [*ago.*]
God. Gode. i. 58. *good.* i. 86. *goods.*
God. [*" A god."* an *exclamatory expression: O god!*]
Gome (grame) *grief, sorrow.*
Gomen. *games, sports.*
Gon. [*go, began to.*]
Goo. [*go.*]
Gost. i. 123. 125. [*guest, person?*]
Goth. *go.*

GLOSSARY.

Goule. par la *goule* de. i. 53. by gods blood. FR.
Gramercy. *thanks.* From
Graunt merci. *many thanks.* FR.
Grate. ii. 169.
Graythed. [*prepared, furnished.*]
Gre. [*prize.*]
Grede. *weep, mourn, lament.*
Gren. [*green.*]
Gresse. [*grass.*]
Greve. *grief.*
Grom. *grooms, men.*
Grucched. [*grudged?*]
Gyn. Gynne. *device or contrivance, snare.*
Gyrd. [*girded.*]
Gyst. *gettest*, [*givest.*]

H.

Ha. Habbe. Habbeth. [*have, hath.*]
Habide. [*abide.*]
Haden. Heden. [*had.*]
Haf ae. *have ay, ever have.*
Hahte. [*hath.*]
Hailsed. [*hailed.*]
Haldes. [*holds.*]
Halewen. Gode halewen. *gods (good?) saints.*
Halt. i. 30. 37. [*helps?*]
Halve. *half, side.*
Ham. *them.*
Hame. [*home.*]
Han. *have.*
Har. Hare. *their.*
Hard. i. 46.
Hardilyche. *hardily resolutely, boldly.*
Hare. i. 45. [*hoary?*]
Haryed. [*plundered, ravaged.*]
Hastifliche. *hastily.*
Hat. i. 83. [*hath.*]
Hat. Hate. i. 44. [*to name or be named.*]
Hattren. *attire, habit, clothes.*
Haved. [*had.*]
Haves. [*have, hath.*]
Hayld. i. 112.
Haylle. i. 98.
Hayward. Haywart. *an inferior officer of a manor or township who had the care of the hedges.*
He. i. 29. *they.* i. 56. *she.* [i. 106. *high.*]
Heal. [*hail.*]
Hear. [*here.*]
Heawyng. [*hewing.*]
Hech. i. 49. [*high?* i. 93. *A low door. A hatch.*]
Heclepyn. [*called.*]
Hede. Heden. *had.*

x 2

Hee. *they.*
Heet. [*called.*]
Hegehen. [*eyes.*]
Hegge. *hedge, thorns.*
Heghe. *high.*
Heh. [*high.*]
Hele. i. 61. [*whole?*]
Hem. *they, them.*
Hemselve. *themselves.*
Hen. On hen. i. 57.
Hende. Hendy. *gentle, civil, courteous.* This *hende.* i. 60. *this kind one.* An *hendy* hap ichabbe yhent. i. 56. *I have caught or gotten a good fortune.*
Hendes. i. 47. [*go?*]
Henne. Hennes. *hence.*
Hent. *taken.*
Hent. Hente. [*to take, catch or receive; took or caught.*]
Heo. *she.*
Her. i. 57. [*hair.* i. 93. *hear.*]
Her. Here. *their.*
Herch. i. 46.
Herie. i. 66.
Herkne. *hearken.*
Herte. [*herd.*]
Heste. i. 59.
Het. *head.*
Heth. i. 70.
Hevede. [*had.*]
Hevedes. *heads.*

Heye. *high.*
Heyse. *ease.*
Hi. [*I.*]
Hight. [*promise.*]
Hii. Hy. *they.*
Him. *they.*
Hinde. [(*hende.*) *gentle, courteous.*]
Hire. Hyre. *her.*
Hirn. i. 43.
Hit. [*It.*]
Hith. i. 42. [*hight, called?*]
Hithte. [*heighth.*]
Ho. Hoo. *who.*
Hode. [*a hood.*]
Hol. *whole.*
Hold. i. 30. [*f. bold.*]
Hold. i. 34. [*held.*]
Hom. [*them.*]
Hond. i. 49. [*hound.*]
Hond. Honde. Honden. [*hand.*] *hands.*
Hondre. Hondrith. [*hundred.*]
Honge. An honge. *hanged.* To honge. *to hang, or be hung.*
Hord. i. 61.
Horin. [*horn.*]
Horribliche. [*horribly.*]
Hosede. i. 70.
Houd. [*behoved.*]
Hour. [*our.*]
Hoved. i. 97. [*hovered.* SAX.]

GLOSSARY.

Hu. Hue. [*he.*] *she. they.*
Huem. *them.*
Huere. i. 29. *their.* [i. 63. *hoar?*]
Huerte. *heart.*
Hulles. *hills.*
Hupe. i. 70.
Husbondes. [*husbandmen.*]
Hy. *they?*
Hye. i. 70.
Hyght. [*promised, undertaken.* On hyght. i. 102. *aloud?*]
Hyphalt. [*halting, lame.*]
Hyre. *her.*

I.

Ibor. i. 74. [*bear?*]
Ibore. *born.*
Ic. [*I.*]
Ich. i. 28. *I.* [i. 91, *each.*]
Ichabbe. *I have.*
Icham. *I am.*
Ichot. *I wot.*
Ichulle. *I shall or will.*
Icumen. *come.*
Ifere. Infere. *together, at once.*
Ifeth. [*in faith.*]
Ihidde. [*hidden.*]
Ilk. Ilke. [*same.*]
Ilka. Ilke. [*each, every.*]
Ilkone. [*each one.*]

Ilor. [*lost.*]
Incontinent. ii. 173.
Interfectours. His *interfectours.* i. 118. *those who killed him.*
Ipocrasie. *hypocrisy.*
Is. *his.*
Isayne. *seen.*
Islawe. [*slain.*]
Iwernd. Noght on *iwernd* nas. i. 75. *not one was unwarned or uninvited.*

J.

Jetted. ii. 180.
Jolyf, *jolly.*
Jugge. *adjudge, sentence.*

K.

Kenne. *see.*
Ketherin. *kerns, Irish-soldiers.*
Keverest. *recoverest.*
Kexis. i. 93.
Kiht. *caught, taken away.*
Kinne. [*kind.* (*kin.*) Caym is *kinne.* i. 75. *Cains kind.*]
Knave. *boy, servant.*
Knulled. i. 54.
Knyth. [*knight.*]
Kreye. *cries.* Kyht. i. 132.
Kyd. [*shewn, seen.*]
Kyn. i. 122.

L.

Kynde. i. 126. [*nature? kin?*]
Kyneriche. *sovereignty.*
Kyneyerde. *sceptre.*
Kyst. *cast.*

L.

Laht. Lauht. Ylaht. *taken.*
Lang. [*long.*]
Lare. [*learning, instruction.* SAX.]
Las. Lasse. *less.*
Lasteles, i. 59.
Lastes, i. 66.
Lat. [*let.*]
Lates. [*lets.*]
Lavyrok. *the lark.*
Layn. [*to conceal, be silent.*]
Leal. [*loyal.*]
Lealte. Leaute. *loyalty, truth, honesty.*
Lebard. [*leopard.*]
Leche. *physician.*
Lede. i. 49.
Lede. Londe and *lede.* i. 55. *land and people, kingdom and subjects.*
Leest. Liest. i. 46. [*lost?*]
Lef. *loving.*
Lefliche. Leflych. *lovely.*
Lemmon, *mistress, sweetheart.*
Lene. [*lend.*]
Lent. i. 56.
Lenten. *lent, spring.*
Leof. *love,* [*as a term of endearment.*] My suete *leof.* i. 62.
Leor. i. 67. [*teach?*]
Lepe. i. 125.
Lerrum. i. 53. [FR. *put?*]
Les. *deceitful, mendacious.*
Lese. [*lose.*]
Leste. [*least.*]
Lete. *forbear, stop, cease.*
Leve. i. 78. l. 1. *believe.* Ib. l. 18. *dear, agreeable.*
Leve. i. 45. [*live?*]
Levedi. Levedy. *lady.*
Levely. i. 67. [*lovely? dear?*]
Lever. i. 101. [*rather, sooner.*]
Lever. i. 122.
Lewde. [*ignorant, unlearned.* SAX.]
Leyde. [*laid.*]
Leyghen. *lay.*
Lhouth. *loweth.*
Lhude. *loud.*
Libbe. [*live,*] *lived.*
Liggen. [*to lye.*]
Liht. i. 67.
Liht. i. 54. [*gay, brisk?*]
Linger. [*longer.*]
Lith. [*active.*]
Lithe. [*listen.*]
Lock. [*look.*]
Loh. *laughed.*

Loht. i. 14. [*loath?*]
Lokkes. *locks (of hair).*
Lomb. *lamb.*
Lome. [He ussid oft ant *lome.* i. 72. The same word and phrase occur in the metrical romance of "Octavian imperator." (Weber. iii. 238.) "The emperour hys sones gan kesse *oft and lome.*"]
Lome. i. 55. Fot-lome. *lame of their feet; unable to make use of their legs for want of their heads.*
Lond. Londe. [i. 24. *land.* i. 66. 101. *the land, country.*]
Lordswyk. *a traitor.*
Lordynges. *sirs, masters.*
Lore. Loren. *lost.*
Lose. *praise.*
Lossom. Lossum. Lussum. *lovesome, lovely.*
Lostlase. i. 70.
Lothen. [*loath.*]
Loute. [i. 92. *loiter.*]
Lovie. [*love.*]
Lowte. [*bow, bend, yield.* SAX.]
Lucettes. i. 101.
Lud. On hyre *lud.* i. 56. *In her own language.*
Luef. [*willing.*]
Lugh. [*laughed.*]
Lumes. *beams.*
Lurcas ende. i. 139.
Lure. lyre. *complexion.*
Lussomore. *lovesomer, lovelier.*
Lust. [*please.* SAX.]
Lustnede. [*pleased.*]
Lustneth. Lystneth. *listen.*
Lut. [*few.*]
Lutel. *little.*
Lyard. i. 14. [*a horse?*]
Lybe. i. 132.
Lyht. *alighted.*
Lyhte. [*contention?* lites. Lat. "And thus he haves her led with *lite.*" Ywaine and Gawin. *is evidently a similar expression, which Mr. Ritson, however, explains "treated with littleness or indifference."*]
Lylie. i. 67.
Lyn. i 67.
Lynde. ["*lime teil*, or *linden-tree;* and hence, figuratively, a tree, or clump of trees, in general."]
Lyven. [*live.*]
Lyver. *livery.*
Lyves man. i. 53.

M.

Ma. i. 46. 50.
Mae. [*more.*]
Magger. [*In spite of.* (*Maugre.*) FR.]
Maistry. Maystry. *power, preeminence, superiority.*
Make. *mate, husband.*
Maked. Makeden. [*made.*]
Man. [*must.*]
Mandeth. i. 64. *mendeth, improveth?*
Mangonel. [*a battering-ram.*]
Mankled. *manacled.*
Mar. Mare. [*more.*]
March-perti. [" *in the parts lying upon the Marches.*" Percy.]
Marke. i. 101.
Mast. [*mayest.*]
Mattes. i. 87.
Mawmentrie. *Mahometanism, idolatry.*
May. *maid, virgin, young woman.*
Mayne. [*strength, force.*]
Meany. [*attendants, servants, retinue.*]
Med. *mead, meadow.*
Mede. *reward.*
Melle. Melle of. *meddle, or have concern with.*

Mene. *moan, grieve, lament.*
Meneth. *moan*[*eth,*] *complain*[*eth.*]
Mensked. i. 43. 44.
Menskful, *graceful, delicate.*
Mer. [*mare.*]
Merchandie. [*merchandise.*]
Merchis. [*marches.*]
Mersh. *March.*
Mest. [*most.*]
Mester. i. 47. [*need?*]
Meve. *move, go, depart.*
Midde. i. 73.
Mihtes. *mightest.*
Mikel. [*much, great.*]
Miles. i. 64.
Mince. ii. 180.
Miri. [*merry.*]
Mithe. [*might, strength.*]
Mo. *more.*
Moch. Moche. [*much, great.*]
Modi. Mody. *the moody or melancholy.*
Mon. ' *man.*'
Mone. *moon.*
Monge. i. 58.
Monie. Mony. Monge. *many.* Other *moni* on. i. 53. *many another one.*
Monimon. *many men.*
Monnes. [*mens.*]

Mo. Moo. [*more.*]
Moren. i. 46. [*morn, morning?*]
Mort. [à mort. i. 106. FR. "The blew *a mort* uppone the bent." *they sounded the death (of the deer) upon the field.*]
Most. [*must.*]
Mot. Mothe. Mouthe. *might.*
Mote. *may.* [*might or must.*]
Mounde. *company, people.* [FR.] With swithe gret mounde. i. 52. *with a very great company; with great numbers of people.*
Mowe. Mowen. *may.*
Mowrmars. *mourners.* [*Perhaps, erroneously, for* mowrnars.]
Moyne. [FR.] *monk.*
Muchele. *much.*
Mucke. *dirt.*
Mulne. [*mill.*]
Mures. Mores. *moors, highlands.*
Murgest. *merriest.*
Murgeth. i. 64. 66.
Murie. *merry.*
Murthes. *mirth.*
Myd. *with.*
Mye. i. 70.
Myht. Myhten. [*might.*]

Mykell. [*great, powerful.*]
Myn. [*mine.*]
Myne-ye-ple. ["*perhaps, many plies, or folds.*" Percy.]
Mysaunter. *misadventure, mischance.*
Myswent. i. 122.

N.

Na. i. 69. *no.* Na down slyt. *does not slide down.* [i. 40. *nor.*]
Naht. *naught, nothing.*
Nappy. ii. 176.
Nare. [*nor.*]
Nath. [*hath not. Probably a mistake in the MS. for* hath.]
Ne. *not.*
Nede. To nede. [*at need.*]
Nedys. [*needs, necessities.*]
Neghe. [*nigh.*]
Neisse. [*foolish. niais.* FR.]
Nelle. *will not.*
Ner. [i. 62. *nearer.* i. 31. *never?*]
Nere. [*were not.*]
Nes. *was not.*
Nete. *horned cattle.*
Nis. Nys. *is not.*
Nith. i. 46. [*night?*]
No. [*nor.*]
Noither. [*neither.*]

Nolde. Nolden. *would not.*
Nollys. [*noddles, heads. nolls.*]
Nome. *name.*
Nome. Nomen. *took.*
None. [*noon.*]
Noneskunnes. i. 55.
Nonys. [for the *nonys. for the nonce, for the purpose or occasion.*]
Noth. [*not; (ne wot,) wot not, know not.*]
Noud. Nout. i. 30. *not.* i. 31. *nothing.*
Noye. i. 92. [*annoyance?*]
Nu. *now.*
Nule. *will not.* Nulle y. i. 62. *will I not.*
Nus ne lerrum en ure. [FR. *We will not put in ure or requisition. Mr. Ritson makes* Nus, " *there is not,*" *and appears unable to attach any meaning to the obscure sentence, which the editor has here attempted to explain.*]
Nyhtegale. [*nightingale.*]
Nythe. *strife, malice, wickedness.*

O.

O. i. 73. a. i. 29. *on.* [i. 69. *one.* i. 67. *ay, ever?*]
Oferlyng. [" *Superior, paramount; opposed to underling.*" Percy.]
Oht. *oath.*
Oither. [*either, or.*]
On. [*in, of, one.*]
On loft. [*aloft.*]
Onane. [*anon.*]
Onde. *contention, fury, wickedness, malice. The precise difference between* nythe *and* onde *cannot be well ascertained.*
Ones. Onys. [*once.*]
Onethe. *scarcely.*
Onfowghten. [*unfought.*]
Oo. i. 63.
Or. *before, ere that.*
Ore. *favour.*
Ost. [*inn.* Ost-house *is still used in the north with this meaning.*]
Oste. *host, army.*
Other, *or.*
Ou. Ow. *you.*
Ous. [*us.*]
Oware. [*hour.*]
Owen. [*own.*]

P.

Pae. [*peacock.*]
Palle. [*fine cloth or silk.*]
Palmer. ii. 197. [*a hermit.*]

GLOSSARY. 315

Pannels. ii. 180.

Parti. Uppone a *parti.* i. 108. [*apart, at a distance.*]

Parvenke. Pervenke. Pervink. *the flower now vulgarly called* periwinkle. [*Parvenche,* FR. Peɲuınce, SAX.]; *but figuratively pink, flower; as used by Shakspeare in the following instances:* "*I am the very pink of courtesy:*"—"*The flower of Europe for his chivalry.*"

Pas pur pas. *step by step.* [FR.]

Passen. [*pass.*]

Pellettes. *balls.*

Peloer. i. 124.

Perde. [*Par dieu.* FR. *An oath frequently used by our early poets, from Chaucer to Shakspeare.*]

Perfit. *perfect.*

Perte. [*part.*]

Pertyd. [*parted, divided.*]

Pes. Pees. *peace.*

Pestilett. *pistol.* See Percys Reliques, i. 120. *This instrument was by no means uncommon about the period in question. In* 1581, *William Bickerton was convicted of the shooting G. Auchinleck of Balmanno with bendit pistolet throu the body.*" Maclaurins *Arguments, &c.* p. 734.

Peyses. [*pieces.*]

Peysse. [*peace.*]

Piete. *pity, compassion, clemency.*

Plawes. i. 66. [*plays?*]

Plesaunce. [*pleasure.*]

Pleyen. [*play.*]

Plow-mell. ["*a small wooden hammer occasionally fixed to the plow, still used in the north: in the midland counties in its stead is used a plow hatchet.*" Percy.]

Pollys. [*polls, heads.*]

Poppynguy. *a parrot,* (*popinjay.*)

Pore. [*poor.*]

Pot. i. 14.

Pouraille. *peasantry, common people, poor.*

Prayse-folk. i. 93. [*The prize-folk. Those who granted the* gre?]

Preseyn. i. 126. *press.* (*Printed, erroneously,* Perseyn.)

Prest. [*prompt, ready.* FR.]

Preve. *prove.*

GLOSSARY.

Pris. Prys. i. 30. i. 32. *prize.* i. 71. *praise, fame.*
Prisone. *prison.*
Prive. [*privy, secret.*]
Profecie. *prophecy. But* Q. *if not a mistake for* Polecie.
Prou. [*advantage.*]
Provant. *food.*
Prude. *pride.*
Prycked. [*rode.* SAX.]
Prye. *look earnestly for.*
Pursue. ii. 70. *track, trail, slot?* " *By the great* pursue *which she there perceav'd.*" Faerie queene, III. v. 28.
Putfalle. *pitfall.*
Pycchynde stake. i. 69. *picking sticks or thorns.*
Pye. i. 70.
Pyght. [*pitched.*]
Pyn. [*pain.*]

Q.
Qualme. i. 47. [*calm?*]
Quean. ii. 173.
Quest. i. 24. [*inquest?*]
Quic. *quick, alive.*
Quite. Quyte. i. 35. *acquit.* [i. 115. *requited, repaid.*] ii. 44. *quit, free, unharmed.*
Quyrry. [*quarry. "in hunting or hawking, is the slaughtered game,* &c.' Percy.]
Quytt. i. 130. *Quytt my* mede. *returned my reward?* [*repaid my love?*]
Qworat. [*whereat.*]

R.
Rad. i. 66. [*advised?*]
Rae. [*roe.*]
Raft. [*reft.*]
Raght. i. 92. [*snatched, seized?*]
Raike. [*range.*]
Rall. i. 99.
Rampande. [*leaping violently.*]
Ran. [*rain.*]
Rapes. i. 48. [*ropes?*]
Rashing. ii. 192. [*rushing?*]
Raught. *stretched.*
Raunsoun. [*ransom.*]
Rayleth. i. 63.
Raysse. [*race.*]
Reames. [*realms.*]
Reane. [*rain.*]
Reas. [*raise.*]
Rechlesse. Rekeless. *reckless, heedless, inattentive.*
Recth. i. 44. 45. [*right?*]
Red. Rede. [i. 55.] i. 66. [122.] *advice.* Token hem to *rede.* i. 38. *took advice with each*

GLOSSARY. 317

other, *consulted together*. [i. 102. *judged*.]
Reddyl. [*a coarse sieve, a riddle.*]
Refe. [*bailiff*.]
Reken. i. 46. [*smoking?*]
Relesse. *relief*. [*release, dismission from pain*.]
Remorse. ii. 203.
Remuy. *remove*.
Rennynge. [*running*.]
Repreve. *reprove*.
Rereth. *reareth, setteth up*.
Res. [*race*.]
Reste. i. 58. [*rested?*]
Retheres hude. i. 35.
Rette. i. 50.
Reu. [*rue*.]
Reve. *steal; or, more properly, rob*. [*reave*.] *Reve me my make*. i. 57. *bereave me of my mistress, take her away from me*.
Rewthe. *pity, compassion*. [*ruth*.]
Rewyth. [*rueth*.]
Ride. [Ful. on *ride*. i. 41. *at full speed?*]
Rod. i. 42. [*rode. pret. of ride*.]
Rode. [i. 58. *the cross, rood*.] i. 63. *colour, complexion*.
Roke. i. 102. [*smoak?*]
Roo. [*roe*.]
Roun. Rounc. *song*. Briddes roune. i. 63. *the song of birds*.
Rouncyn. *a horse of an inferior size or quality, a common labouring horse*.
Rounes. i. 64.
Rourh. Whare *rourh*. i. 51. *a mistake, perhaps, for whare* thourh, *or* throuh, *by reason whereof*.
Route. i. 138. *about, round*.
Rugged. [" *pulled with violence*." Percy.]
Rybaus. *ribalds, rascals*.
Ryhte. *right*.
Rymith. i. 45.
Rymittes. i. 44.
Rynde. i. 101.

S.

Sa. [i. 48. *discourse, saw*. i. 92. *so*.]
Sacryng. *elevation of the host, when a little bell is rung, called the* sacring *bell*.
Saht. i. 30. 67.
Saisede. [*seized, took*.]
Sall. Salle. [*shall*.]
Sample. *example*.
Sanchothis. i. 84.
Sar. Sare. [*sore*.]

GLOSSARY.

Sauf. *save.*
Sauntz. *(sans.* FR.*) without.*
Sawe. *speech, discourse.* Seiden so in *sawe.* i. 29. *made a common saying of it.*
Say. [*saw. The preterit of* see.]
Sayne. [*say.*]
Scant. ii. 169.
Scheldys. [*shields.*]
Schent. *ruined, undone.* See Shent.
Schette. i. 84. Schoote. i. 99. [*shot. The pret. of shoot.*]
Schote. [*shoot.*]
Schrogen. i. 46. [*shrubs?*]
Schul. Schulle. *shall.*
Scomfet. [*discomfit.*]
Scort. [*short.*]
Scote. *shot,* [*payment.* FR. *scot.*]
Scoyer. Scwyer. Swyer. *squire.*
Seche. *seek.*
Sed. *seed.*
See. Set in *see.* i. 31. *set in seat; set upon a throne; thus we still say, the* see *of Rome, Canterbury, &c.* [*Sedes,* Lat.]
See. i. 32. *regard, keep in his sight.*
Segge. *say.*

Seghe. *to look.*
Seiden. *said.*
Seien. *say.*
Seind. i. 67. [*sent?*]
Sek. [*a sack.*]
Seker. *sure.*
Sekyrly. *certainly.*
Seld. Selde. *seldom.*
Seli. [*silly, foolish.*]
Selkethe. A *selkethe* wyse. i. 36. *of a strange shape or fashion.*
Selthe. i. 67.
Selven. [*self.*]
Semlohest. *seemliest.*
Sen. [*since.*]
Send. Sende. *sent.*
Seo. [*see.*]
Serewe. *sorrow.*
Sesoyne. *Saxony.*
Seten. i. 34. [*sitting?*]
Sethen. [*since.*]
Seththe. [*afterwards.*]
Sey. [*say.*]
Shent. Thus to be *shent.* ii. 5. *To be thus disgraced, to be brought to this shameful end.* [*part. pass. of* shend.]
Shereth. i. 69.
Shoddreth. [*shuddereth.*]
Shome. *shame.*
Shonde. ii. 36.
Shonkes. [*shanks.*] Whil him.

GLOSSARY.

lesteth the lyf with the longe shonkes. i. 38. *so long as he with the long shanks lives;* i. e. *K. Edward I. so called from the length of his legs.*
Shope. *made.*
Shreward. i. 14. [*rascal?*]
Shulden. [*should.*]
Shule. *shall.*
Shup. [*shaped.*]
Shurtyng. [*" recreation, diversion, pastime."* Percy.]
Sides. i. 43. [*decide?*]
Sigge. *say.*
Sike. Siked. *sighed.*
Sikernes.[*league, confederacy.*]
Site. *city.*
Sithen. [*then.*]
Siwed. i. 60. [*served?*]
Slaye. [*slain.*]
Sleeche. i. 46. [*cunning?*]
Slo. *slay.*
Slon. To slon. *To be slain.*
Sloughe. [*slew.*]
Slowen. [*slew.*]
Slyt. *slide.*
Smerte. [*smart.*]
Smot. i. 55. [*hung?*]
Smyte. Of smyte. i. 34. *smitten of.*
So. [*as.*] *So* liht. *so.* i. 54. *as light as.*

Sodeyn. [*sudden.*]
Soffid. [*sought.*]
Soht. i. 31. *sooth, truth.* [i. 60. *sought?*]
Sojoure. [*sojourn.*]
Solsecle. *sunflower,* solsequium.
Son. [*soon.*]
Sond. [*gift.*]
Sonde. Godes *sonde.* i. 38. [*Gods messenger; the Messiah.*]
Soot. i. 41.
Sori. [*sorry.*]
Sot. i. 14.
Souse. ii. 175.
South. [i. 43. *sooth, sweet, delightful.* i. 48. *truth.*]
Spendyd. i. 112. [*" probably the same as spanned, grasped."* Percy.]
Spene. *spend.* Spene bred. i. 54. *consume victuals; i. e. keeping thee in prison would be expensive to us.*
Spens. [*expense.*]
Spired. [*enquired.*]
Sporeles. [*spur-less.*]
Spray. *sprigs.*
Sprente. [*spurted, sprung out.*]
Springen, i. 53. [*spread?*]
Spurn. *See* Tear.
Stage. [*stag.* Styrande many

GLOSSARY.

a *stage.* i. 95. "*A friend interpreted this*" (*says dr. Percy*) "*many a stirring travelling journey!*"]

Stalworth. [*strong, stout, lusty;* " *And* stalworth *knight als stele.*" R. of Brunne.]

Stan. Stane. [*stone.*]

Starres. i. 101. *Erroneously printed* stanes. *stars.*

Stat. [*state.*]

Stede. Stid. *place.* (*stead.*)

Stel. i. 13.

Sterne. i. 110. [*fiercely?* SAX.]

Sterteth. i. 11. [*leaps about, gambols?*]

Stevenyng. i. 67. [*speaking, speech?*]

Stond. stont. *stands.*

Stonde. Stounde. *space of time, more or less.*

Stoore. i. 74.

Stour. Stoure. Stowre. [*battle, contest, assault.*]

Stra. [*straw.*]

Streit. i. 69.

Strem. [*stream.*]

Stret. [*street.*]

Strides. i. 41.

Striketh. i. 64. [*passeth?* ꝼꞃꞃeccan. SAX.]

Stude. *place.*

Styrande. i. 95. [*stirring, disturbing?*]

Styrt. [*started.*]

Suar. [*sure?*]

Suerd. Swerde. [*swords.*]

Suereth. *swear.*

Suet. *sweet.*

Suetyng. [*sweeting. A term of endearment.*]

Sugge. *say.*

Suilk. Suilke. [*such.*]

Suithe. Suythe, Swithe. *very, full.*

Sul. [*shall.*]

Suld. [*should.*]

Sumer. *summer.*

Sunne. *sin.*

Surreccion. [*insurrection.*]

Suyre. Swyre. *neck.*

Swa. [*so.*]

Swapped. i. 102. 103. [*struggled, fought, exchanged blows?*]

Swenne. i. 47.

Swepyllys. ["*A* sweped *is that staff of the flail with which the corn is beaten out, vulg. a* supple." Percy.]

Sweyn. *man.* ["*Some kind of inferior servant.*" Met. Rom.]

Swik. *cease.*

Swon. *swan.*

GLOSSARY.

Swote. i. 61. [*sweet?*]
Swyke. [*deceit.*]
Swykedom. *deceit, treachery.*
Swynkers. [*labourers.*]
Swyppyng. [*striking.* Swipe is still used in the North in the same sense.]
Swyvyng. l. 12.
Syde. [*long.*]
Syk. *sigh.*
Sykyng. *sighing.*
Syne. [i. 96. *since.* i. 97. 102. *then.*]
Sytht. i. 69. [*saw?*]
Syx-menys-sang. i. 94.

T.

Ta. [*take.*]
Tahte. [*taught.*]
Tane. [*the one.*]
Tayne. taen. [*taken.*]
Te. [*to.*]
Tear. i. 115. [*this seems to be a proverb.* " *That* tearing *or* pulling *occasioned this* spurn *or* kick." Percy.]
Teh. i. 70.
Temed. i. 30.
Tene. i. 51. *ten.* i. 62. *grieve.* [i. 23. *ill-will.*]
Teone. i. 70.
Ternement. *torment.* [*torture.*] *martyrdom.*

Thah. i. 36. *though.* [i. 92. *them.*]
Than. [*then.*]
Tharinne. [*therein.*]
Thart. [*thou art.*]
The. i. 36. *thrive.* [i. 14. *thou.* i. 35. 83. *thee.* i. 106. *they.*]
Theem. [*them.*]
Theghes. *thighs.*
Then. [*than.*]
Thenche. *think.*
Ther. *where.*
Theynes. i. 32.
Thi. [*they.*]
Thideward. *thitherward.*
This. *these.*
Tho. i. 30. ii. 189. *then.* i. 35. *when.* i. 60. *those.*
Thoht. Thohte. [*thought.*]
Tholien. [*From* thole. *to suffer, endure.*] Betere is *tholien* whyle sore then mournen evermore. i. 57. *it is better to suffer a temporary evil than to mourn for ever.*
Thonke. *thank.*
Thonkes. i. 38.
Thouche. [*though.*]
Thourh. [*through.*]
Thouth. [*thought.*]
Thrange. [*throng.*]
Thrat. *threatens.*

VOL. II. Y

Thred. [*third.*]
Threstelcoc. *throstle, thrush.*
Threteth. i. 63.
Thritti-thousent.[*thirty thousand.*]
Throwe. *thrown.*
Thrumme. *a thrum is the fringed end of a weavers web.*
Thrustand. i. 89.[*thrusting?*]
Thrye. i. 30.
Thunche. *think.*
Thurh. *through.*
Til. [*to.*]
To. [i. 66. 67. *too.* i. 98. *two.*]
Toc. [*took.*]
To-drawe. [*drag away, draw.*]
To-drowe. [*drawn.*]
To-flatred. i. 91. [*flattened?*]
To-foren. [*before.* SAX.]
Token. *took, gave.*
Tokenyng. i. 88. [*token, keepsake?*]
Tome. i. 55. [*tame? toom.* (*empty.*)]
Tone. [*the one.*]
To-schatred. [*shattered, broken in pieces.*]
To-slatred. ["*slit, broke into splinters.*" Percy.]
To-tereth. [*teareth.*]
Totowe. *too, too.*
Touch. ii. 158.
Toupe. [*tup.*]

To-yeynes. *against.*
Tprot. *trut. an ejaculation of contempt.* (*Used by* Robert of Brunne.)
Trai. [*betray.*]
Tre. [*tree, wood.*]
Trechour. [*a deceiver.* FR.]
Tremuleth. [*trembleth.*]
Trichard. [*treacherous.*]
Tricthen. [*trick.*]
Trippand. [*tripping.*]
Triste. i. 35. [*trust? sad?*]
Trone. [*throne.* FR.]
Trou. Trowe. [*believe, trow.*]
Trous. [i. 69. l. 15. *holes.* l. 25. *trousers.* FR.]
Trouth-plyght. [*plighted, faith.*]
Trouthe. [*troth, truth.*]
Trowe. [*trow.* "*An exclamation of inquiry.*" Johnson. Perhaps, trow-ye.]
Trusyd. [*trussed.*] *Trykare. ii. 32.*
Tubrugge. i. 37.
Twa. Twaw. [*two.*]
Twattling. ii. 182.
Twybyl. *bill, hedge-bill.*
Twedges. *twigs.*
Tyne. i. 46. [*to burn?*]
Tything. i. 47. [*tidings?*]

U.

Uch. *each.*
Umbestounde. i. 67.

GLOSSARY.

Underfynde. i. 66.
Undergore. i. 57.
Ur. *our.*
Ure. i. 53. [FR. *requisition?*]
Ute. [*out.*]

V.

Valle. [*fall.*]
Vent. [*went.*]
Verament. [*verily, truly.* FR.]
Verteth. *goeth to harbour in the* vert *or fern.* Sir J. Hawkins. Q.
Vicome. i. 39.
Villiche. *vilely.*
Vones. [*once.*]
Vor. [*for.*]
Vrenshe. [*French.*]
Vyhte. i. 38. [*fight?*]
Vylte. *ill-usage,* [*villany.* FR.]
Vytouten. [*without.*]

W.

Wa. [i. 46. *woe?* i. 50. *woful.* i. 44. *who.*]
Wache. [*guard, sentinel.*]
Wajour. *wager.*
Wald. [*would.*]
Wane. [i. 42. *plenty?* i. 111. *one?*]
War. Ware. Warre. [i. 44. 92. *be, were.* i. 67. 120. *beware; wary, prudent.*]

Ware. i. 54. [*warisoun, reward?*]
Warny. *warn, give warning or notice to.*
Waron. i. 35. [*were?*]
Waryed. [*accursed.*]
Waryson. [*hire, reward.*]
Wat. Wate. [i. 109. *wot, know.* i. 45. *what.*]
Waxe. Waxen. Waxeth. *grow.*
Wayte. i. 45. [*await? serve?*]
Waytes. [*sentinels, watchmen.*]
W[o]de. *wood.*
Weal. i. 115. [*wail.* Percy.]
Webbes. *websters, weavers.*
Wed. Wede. *weed, clothes.*
Wedde. *gage, pledge, pawn.*
Weht. [*what.*]
Wel. i. 53. *very.* [i. 55. *will.*]
Weld. [*wield, govern.*]
Wele. i. 63.
Welke. [*which.*]
Wen. [i. 45. *when.* i. 49. *ween, think.*]
Wende. i. 52. 100. [*wend.*] *go.*
Wende. i. 57. [*Perhaps ween, think, ponder.*]
Wende. Wenden. Went. *weened, thought.*
Wentyn. [*went.*]
Weolc. i. 64.

Werde. i. 48. [*worthy?*]
Were. Werre. [*war.*]
Weren. Wern. [*were.*]
Werrure. [*warrior.*]
Wes. [*was.*]
Wet. Whet. *what.*
Wext. *waxed, grown.*
Weylaway. Weylawo. [*woe! alas!* SAX.]
Whittol. *whittle, knife.*
Whittore. *whiter.*
Whose. *whoso; a dissyllable.*
Wild. [*would.*].
Wilk. [*which.*]
Willerdome. i. 126. *wilfulness?*
Wist. Wiste. [*knew. (the preterit of* wis.)]
Wit. Wyt. [*with.*]
Witte. *know.*
Wlyteth. i. 63.
Wo. [i. 63. *gone?* i. 114. *woful, sad.*]
Wod. i. 32. [*went?*]
Woderove. i. 63. [*a bird? a plant?*]
Woh. [*wo.*]
Wolde. [*would.*]
Wolle. Wolleth. *will.*
Wolt. Chryst *wolt.* ii. 22. *would to Christ.*
Won. i. 57. [*cheeks.*] i. 58. *habitation.* i. 61. *wan.* (*pale.*) ii. 5. *wont, practice, custom.*
Wone. [i. 48. *go.* i. 113. *one.*]
Wonges. [*cheeks.*]
Woninge-stede. [*dwelling-place.*]
Wonne. [*abide.*]
Woo. [*wo.*]
Worche. *work, act.*
Wore. i. 57.
Worhliche. Wurliche. i. 59.
Worly. i. 66. [*worthy?*]
Wormes. *serpents.*
Worth. i. 43.
Wost. [*wottest, knowest.*]
Wouche. [*mischief, evil.* þohȝ. SAX.]
Wounder. *wondrous.*
Wowe. i. 77. [*wall or window (of the church)?*]
Wowes. i. 64. *woo.* [i. 123. *windows.*]
Woweth. *wooeth.*
Wowing. [*wooing.*]
Wrang. [i. 47. *wrong.* i. 92. *jostled, squeezed. The pret. of* wring.]
Wrangwis. [*wrongous.*]
Wroth. [*wrought.*]
Wunne. i. 35. [*won, gained?* i. 64. *dwelling, residence, lodging.*]

GLOSSARY.   325

Wurliche. i. 58.
Wyht. i. 34. *man, person.*
i. 64. *quite, wholly, altogether.* Q.
Wyise. *wish.*
Wymmen. Wymmon. [*women.*]
Wyn. i. 53. [*go?*]
Wynde. See Wende.
Wynne. [i. 87. "*Brouke hur wyth* wynne." "*Enjoy her with pleasure.*" Percy. i. 94. *win, gain, get?* i. 98. *gain, profit.*]
Wyrch. [*work.*]
Wys. [*wise.*]
Wysloker. *wiser, more wisely.*
Wyspes. [*wisps.*]
Wyste. [*knew.*]
Wyt. [i. 42. *knowledge.* i. 43. *with.*]
Wyte. i. 34. *know.* i. 37. *guard.* [i. 41. *white.*]
Wyter. *wise, knowing.*
Wythe. [*wise.*]
Wythouten. [*without.*]

X.

Xal. Xalt. *shall, shalt.*
Xul. *shall.*

Y.

Y. I. *in.*

Yarked yare. *prepared ready.*
Yate. [*gate.*]
Yatid. i. 43.
Ybate. i. 34.
Ybe. [*been.*]
Yboren. [i. 13. *carried, borne.*
i. 69. *born.*]
Ybounde. *bound.*
Ybrend. *burned.*
Ycaht. *caught.*
Ych. [*same.*]
Ychalbe. *I shall be.*
Yche. [*each.*]
Ychot. *I wot.*
Ycome. [*come.*]
Ycore. *chosen.*
Ycud. i. 29.
Ydemed. *judged, sentenced.*
Ydon. i. 56. [*put?*]
Ydyht. *dight, dressed, set, placed, put.*
Yede. Yod. Yode. [*went.*]
Yef. Yefe. *if.*
Yefeth. i. 115. [*in faith?*]
Yeghe. i. 70.
Yelpe. *yelp, boast.*
Yeme. i. 31. *exercise?*
Yer. Yere. Yeris. *year, years.*
Yere. *ere, before.*
Yering. i. 43.
Yerlle. [*each.*]
Yeu. *you.*
Yeve. Yewe. Yive. *give.*

GLOSSARY.

Yeyn. i. 67.
Yfed. [*fed.*]
Yfetered. [*fettered.*]
Yhent. *caught, or gotten.*
Yherde. Yherden. *heard.*
Yhere. [*here.*]
Yheryed. i. 59.
Yis. [*is.*]
Yiftes. [*gifts.*]
Yite. [*yet.*]
Yknawe. *know.*
Yknowe. [*known.*]
Ylaht. [*pret. of* latch.] *taken; as in a net or snare.* [*caught.*]
Ylent. i. 57.
Yloren. *lost.*
Ymak. *made.*
Yn. *inn.*
Ynemned. *named.*
Ynoh. *enough.*
Ynuste. *I wish not.*
Yol. *Yule. Christmas.*
Yolden. [*holden.*]
Yonde-alf. [*yonder half.*]
Yone. *yon.*
Yongeth. i. 31. *singeth?* [*Perhaps* Gongeth, *goeth; from the Saxon* ȝonȝan, *to go.*]
Yore. [*long.*]
Yoven. Yovyn. *given. The word* yoven *is still retained in the leases granted by the dean and chapter of Westminster.*
Yoye. *joy.*
Yplyht. [*plighted.*]
Ypreye. *I pray.*
Yrn. Yrnene. *iron.*
Ys. i. 13. *his.*
Yslake. i. 61.
Ysoht. [*sought.*]
Ysped. [*sped.*]
Ystyked. *sticked.*
Ysuore. [*sworn.*]
Ytake. [*taken.*]
Yth. [*i' th,' in the.*]
Ytuht. i. 35.
Yut. [*yet.*]
Yvel. [*evil.*]
Ywaxe. [*waxeth, groweth.*]
Ywraht. Ywroht. *wrought, formed.*
Y-yyrned. i. 57.

THE END.

Index.

Index.

A Becket, Thomas, archbishop of Canterbury. I. 16.
Abel, Sir John. I. 35.
"Aldingar, Sir". xxix.
Alfred and An Caff, Stories of. iii.
Ambree, Mary. xcix.
Anthony Now-Now. lxxvii. lxxxix. II. 273 et seq.
Armada, the Spanish. II. 280 et seq.
Armstrong, John. II. 214 et seq.
Arthur, King. iii.
Artois, Earl of. I. 51 et seq.
"As at noon Dulcina rested". II. 268.
"As blind as a harper". lvii et seq.
Ashwell, a musician. lxxiii.
Asheton, William. II. 38.
Athol, Earl of. I. 37.

Aylmer de Valence. I. 32.

Baldwin, John. lxxxi.
Ballads, Names of old. lxxxii et seq. lxxxix. xcix.
Bamborough shire. I. 95 et seq.
Bannockburn, Battle of. xlviii.
Bartholomeus De Proprietatibus Rerum. lxiv.
"Battle of Otterbourne, the." xxxii.
Bayonne. I. 119.
Beaumont and Fletcher. xcvi. II. 64 et seq.
"Beggar's daughter of Bethnal-Green, the." xxx.
"Beginning of the world, the," a tune. xx.
Belfour. I. 25.
Belregard, Bois de. I. 24 et seq.
Bennet, John. I. 11.
Berwick on Tweed. I. 96.
Bigod, Hugh, earl of Norfolk. xli.
"Birth of St George, the." xxxi.
Blacklock, Dr. ci.
Blondel de Neale. v.
Bold, Henry. II. 218.

Boleyn, Anne. II 275.
Booker, John. II. 258 et seq.
Bordeaux. I. 149.
Botiler, Sir Edmund. I. 73.
Boulogne. II. 273 et seq.
Boulogne, Earl of. I. 53.
Boulogne, St Anne of. II. 273 et seq.
Bradley, A. II. 268.
Brathwaite, Richard. lxvi.
Braintree fair. xc.
Brakley, John. liii.
Breton, Nicholas. li.
Bruce, Robert. I. 28 et seq.
Burges. I. 51 et seq.
Bull-running of Tuthury. xi et seq.
Bungay, Castle of. xli.

Calais. I. 153. II. 253. 273.
Cambridge. II. 284.
"Candlemas Day", a mystery. xxi.
Captain Cox. xxxii et seq. II. 38 et seq.

Carlisle, Bishop of. I. 119.
Carols. lvi. I. 140 et seq. II. 114 et seq. 238 et seq.
"Cauline, Sir". xxix.
Chalkhill, John. II. 51.
Charing cross. II. 254 et seq.
Charles's wain. II. 258.
Chatelain, George. I. 144.
Chaucer. xxii. xlv et seq. lvii. lix. lxiii et seq.
Cheap. I. 36.
Chester. V et seq.
Chester plays. II. 8.
Chettle, Henry. lxxxix.
Cheviot, Hunting of the. I. 105 et seq.
Chevy-chase. xxxii. xxxiv. II. 218 et seq.
"Child of Elle, the." xxix.
Child Rowland. xciv.
Christmas. lvi. I. 140. II. 114 et seq. 238 et seq.
"City Mouse and Country Mouse", a fable. xci.
Clifton, in Nottingham. II. 95 et seq.
Clyde to Clare. I. 46.
Cockney, King of. xli.

Coke's "Reports." II. 284.

Colgrin, Story of. iii.

"Colle to me the rysshys grene", a song. lxxv et seq.

Cologne, King of. II. 273.

"Come, shepherds, deck your heads." II. 268.

"Complaynt of Scotland." lix. lxv. lxxxiv.

Compton, Sir Francis. II. 290.

Coning, Peter. I. 52.

Copland, Wr. I. 132.

Coppeld, the name of a horse. I. 87.

Cornhill. II. 276.

Cornysh, a musician. lxxiii.

Cotton, Charles. lviii. xcviii.

Cowper, Dr. lxxiii.

Cromwell, Thomas, lord. xcviii.

Crowd. lxi et seq.

Crowder, Blind. xxxiv.

Cuckoo, Song of the. I. 10 et seq.

Cyprus. I. 154.

Dade, an almanac-maker. II. 258 et seq.

Dance-tunes, Names of old. li.

Dancing. lvii.

Davie, Adam. lxiv.

De la Pole, William, duke of Suffolk. I. 117 et seq.

Deloney, Thomas. xx. xxii. xc. xcviii et seq. II. 70 et seq. 106. 120. 126. 188. 273.

Devel, Sir Ralph. I. 53.

"Disobedient Child." xx.

"Donkin Dargison", a tune. II. 44.

Douglas, Earl of. I. 91 et seq. 105 et seq. II. 219 et seq.

Douglas, Sir James a. I. 103.

Dove, an almanac-maker. II. 258 et seq.

Dover. I. 14. II. 253. 273 et seq. 281.

Drake, Sir Francis. II. 281.

Drincheil. xlvii et seq.

Dryden's Miscellany. xxxii.

Dudley, Baron of. I. 120.

Dunbar, Battle of. xliii et seq. I. 28 et seq.

D'urfey, Tom. lviii. xcvi. II. 55. 247. 268. 280.

Dutton of Dutton. viii et seq.

Earle, Bishop. II. 57.

"Eastward hoe", a play. II. 47.
Edgecumbe family. II. 15.
Edom o' Gordon. II. 38 et seq.
Edward I. x. xliv. lxxxvii. I. 14. 16. 28 et seq. II. 254.
Edward II. I. 32. 56.
Edward III. xviii.
Edward IV. xviii.
Edward VI. xix. lxxx et seq.
Elderton, William. xc et seq. xcv. xcvii et seq.
Eldon, Lord. I. 4.
Elizabeth, Queen. xiv. xxvi. xxxiv. lxxxii. II. 281.
Ellis, George. I. 18.
"English Mall." xcix.
Etienne de Procaire. I. 150.
Evesham, Battle of. I. 15.
Exchange, The. II. 276.

"Fair Margaret and Sweet William". xxxii. II. 92 et seq.
Faversham, Earl of. II. 291.
Fayrfax, Dr. lxxiii.
Fiddle. lxi et seq.

Fiddlers. xxi.
Fiddlers, Act against. xxiii et seq.
Fiddlers and shoemakers. vii et seq.
Fife, Earl of. I. 95.
Fitz-Hugh, Sir John. I. 104.
Fitz-thomas, Sir John le. I. 73.
Flamborough. I. 81.
Flemings. I. 51 et seq.
Flodden, Battle of. II. 70 et seq.
"Four Elements, the", a morality. lxxii et seq.
Freemen's Songs. lxxix et seq. II. 54. 57 et seq.
French, Ballad against the. I. 51 et seq.
French minstrels. xvii.
French poetry. iv. xlv.
Frisell, Sir Simon. I. 28 et seq.

"Gammer Gurton's Needle." lxxxviii.
Gandalin. I. 81 et seq.
Gilboie. I. 74.
Giles de Bretagne. I. 148.
Glasgow, Bishop of. I. 30.

Gloucester, Duke of. I. 148.
Gloucester, Earl of. I. 16.
Gosson, Stephen. li.
Gower, John. xlv. lx.
Graistoke, Baron of. I. 100.
Gray, William. lxxvii.
Gray's Inn. II. 284.
Green-Leyton. I. 95.
Greene, Robert. xxi.
Grove, Matthew. xxiii.
Gwynneth, John. lxxiii.
Gysborn, John. II. 7.

H
Halidon-Hill, Battle of. xviii.
Hamilton, Lord. II. 48.
Hammond, an almanac-maker. II. 259 et seq.
Harbottel, Sir James. I. 104.
Harrison, Robert, of Durham. I. 4.
Harsnet, Samuel, archbishop of York. cii.
Harley, Sir Roger. I. 113.
Harvy Hafter. lxx et seq.

Hawkill, John. xlvii.
Hawkins, Sir John. I. 10 et seq. etc.
"Heir of Linne, the." xxx. I. 81.
Hengist. xlix.
Henry II. xli. xliii.
Henry III. xliii. I. 12.
Henry VI. lxix. I. 128.
Henry VII. lxxxv.
Henry VIII. xiii. xix. li. lxxvii. lxxix. lxxxi. lxxxiii. II. 273 et seq.
Herbert of Norham, Sir. I. 34.
Heron, Sir William. I. 113.
Hewitt, Richard. ci.
"Hey Robin, jolly Robin", a song. xciii.
Hogarth, William. xx. lix.
Hornpipes of Cornouaille. li. lxv et seq.
Hugh de Bigot. I. 13.
Hugh de Dutton. vi.
Hugh le Despenser. I. 15 et seq.
Humber. I. 43.
"Hunt is up, the", a song. lxxvii et seq.
Huntly, Earl of. I. 98.

Hurdy-gurdy. lx.
Husband the discontented. II. 36 et seq.
Hutton, Henry. XXIII.

Irish, the. I. 70 et seq.
Islington. II. 134 et seq.
Ivy and Holly. I. 131 et seq.

Jack H——ls, the harper. lviii.
Jack Napes. I. 117 et seq.
Jack of Newbury. XX.
Jack the Giant Killer. XCIV.
James I. of Scotland. I. 146.
Joan, countess of Toulouse. I. 8.
"Joan of France". XCIX.
"John Armstrong." XXXII et seq.
John Dory. XXXII et seq. XXXV. lxxix. II. 57 et seq.
John of Agurstone, Sir. I. 99 et seq.
John of Gaunt. XI.
Johnson, Richard. XCVII. XCIX. C.
Johnson, Robert. II. 51.

Jones, R., a musician. lxxiii.
Jonson, Ben. xxiii. lviii. II. 238.
Jordan, Thomas. II. 282.
José, Sir John. I. 33.

Kethe, William. II. 31 et seq.
"Kind-Harts Dream." lxxvii. lxxxix.
"King Arthur's death." xxxi.
"King Henry's Mirth." lxxix. II. 54.
King Hobbe. I. 31.
"King Lear." lxxxv. xciv.
King of the Minstrels. xi et seq.
King's Note, the. lix.
Kirkencliff, Battle of. I. 28 et seq.
Knight of the Sun. II. 280.
Knouille. I. 25.

"Labandula shot?" See opposite.
Lampe. I. 11.
Laneham's Letter. xv. lxxxii.
Langland, William. xvi. xix. lxii. II. 8.
Langston, Lt Col. II. 290.

Langtoft, Peter. xliv. I. 22.

Le Grand, M. ii. lx.

Liard, Walter. I. 119.

"Little Musgrave and Lady Barnard." xxxii et seq. I. History.

Lollards. I. 121 et seq.

London bridge. I. 28 et seq.

"London Lyckpeny." lviii.

"Lord Thomas and fair Eleanor." xxvi. xxxii et seq. II. 89 et seq.

Lordal, Sir David. I. 114.

Louis XI. of France. II. 275.

Lovel, Lord. lxxxv.

Lovel, Sir George. I. 113.

"Lusty Juventus." xxi. lxxx.

Lydgate, John. I. 128.

Lyly, John. xxi. lvii.

Lyndesy, Sir John of. I. 32.

Lyth, Robin. I. 81 et seq.

"Labendula shott," a tune. II. 47

Mac Mal More, Ethe. I. 74.

Man in the moon. I. 68 et seq.

Mannington, George. II. 147 et seq.

Mannyng, Robert. xliv. I. 22.

Map, Walter. I. 3.

⎡ Margaret of Scotland. II. 15.
⎣ Margaret, duchess of Burgundy. lxxxv.

Marlowe, Christopher. xci.

"Marriage of Sir Gawaine". xxx.

Martin, Tom, of Palgrave. liii.

Martyn. I. 25.

Mary, the Virgin. liv et seq.

Maxwell, Sir Hugh. I. 104. 114.

Medina Sidonia, Duke of. II. 280.

Montague, Earl of. I. 98. 103.

Merlin. xvi.

Mickleton, James. II. 31.

Minstrels, the ancient English. i et seq.

"Mirrour of Knighthood, the." II. 280.

Molines. I. 119.

Molinet, Jean. I. 144. 156.

Montgomery, Sir Hugh. I. 105. 111 et seq. II. 225 et seq.

Morte Arthur. xv. xxxi.

Munday, Anthony. lxxxix. xcviii.
Murray, Sir Charles. I. 104. 114.
Music, Ancient English. xxxix et seq.
Music, Specimen of, from an early MS. liv et seq.
Musical instruments, Ancient. lvii et seq.

Naples. I. 151 et seq.
Nash, Thomas. xc.
"New Academy of Compliments, The." II. 286.
Newcastle-upon-Tyne. I. 95 et seq.
Newgate. I. 33.
Noel. II. 16 et seq.
Normandy. I. 150.
Northumberland. I. 95 et seq. 105 et seq. I. 75 et seq.

O'Connor. I. 74.
"Old Simon the King." lxxxii.
Oldcastle, Sir John, lord Cobham. I. 121.
Orleans, Charles, duke of. lxvii.
Orleans, Siege of. I. 145.
Otterbourne, Battle of. I. 74 et seq.

Oatneap-hill. I. 95.

Paris-Garden. II. 255.
Parker, Martin. II. 257 et seq. 263.
Parma, Prince of. II. 281.
Partridge, an almanac-maker. II. 261.
Paston, John. I. 117.
Paston, Sir William. liii.
Peele, George. lxxxvii.
Penny, Sir. I. 134 et seq.
Pepusch, Dr. xc.
Percy, Bishop. i et seq.
Percy, Sir Harry. I. 95 et seq. 105 et seq. II. 218 et seq.
Philip Augustus, King of France. I. 7.
Philip the Fair. I. 51 et seq.
Philip II. of Spain. II. 281.
Piers of Birmingham, Sir. I. 70 et seq.
Placebo and Dirige. I. 117 et seq.
Playford, John. lxii.
Plough, John. II. 32.
"Plowman's Tale, the." xlvii.

Pond, an astrologer. II. 258 et siq.
Puttenham, George. lxxvii. lxxxvii.
Pygot, a musician. lxxiii.

"Queen Dido." c.

Ralph of Sandwich, Sir. I. 34.
Randal Blundeville, earl of Chester. v et seq. xlvi.
Ravenscroft. II. 53.
Repailles. I. 146.
Richard I. iv et seq. I. 6 et seq.
Richard II. xi.
Richard, King of the Romans. xliii. 12 et seq.
Rimo, an almanac-maker. II. 258 et seq.
Robert of Gloucester. xlviii.
Robin Hood. xlvi. I. 81.
"Robin, lend to me thy bow." II. 69 et seq.
Rochford, George, viscount. II. 12.
Rodecliff orag. I. 95.
Roger (or John) de Lacy, Constable of Chester. vi.
Roos. I. 119.

Rosin, Old father. xxiii.

Rouen. I. 145 et seq.

"Row the boat, Norman, row." lxx et seq.

Rowland. xciv.

St Albans, Abbot of. I. 119.

St Albans, Battle of. lxix.

St Andrews, Bishop of. I. 30.

St David's, Bishop of. I. 119.

St Edmund's day. I. 143.

St James. I. 148.

St Pol, Sir Jacques de. I. 52 et seq.

St Stephen's day. I. 141.

Sampson, William. II. 95.

Say, John. I. 119 et seq.

"Schole House of Women, the". lxiv.

Scone, Abbot of.. I. 30.

Scots, Ballads against the. I. 28 et seq.

Scott, Sir David. I. 99 et seq.

Scott, Sir Walter. I. 157.

Sellenger's Round. li.

Shakspeare. r. xxiii. lviii. lxvi. xc. xci et seq. c. I. 63. II. 60 et seq. 64.

Silk, Capt. II. 258.

Simon de Montfort. I. 13. 15 et seq.

Skelton, John. xix. lxiii et seq. lxx et seq. I. 117. II. 71.

Song, Drinking. xlix et seq.

Songs, An ancient book of. lxxiii et seq.

Songs, Love. liv.

Song-writing. lxvii et seq.

Spenser, Edmund. xxii. lx.

Spigurnal, Henry. I. 25.

"Squyr of Lowe degre, the." lxiii.

Sternhold, Thomas. lxxxi.

Steward, Sir Walter. I. 99 et seq.

Stowell, Lord. I. 4.

"Summer and the Winter, a poem upon the contention between the." I. 132.

Surrey, Earl of. lxiv. xc.

Swallow, an almanac-maker. II. 258 et seq.

Sweet, Martin. lxxxiv et seq.

Tamar, a musician. lxxiii.

"Theatre of Compliments, the." I. 268. 286.

Theobald of Pevanes. I. 39.
Thomas of Ersildon. lxviii.
Thomas of Multon, Sir. I. 33 et seq.
Threadneedle street. II. 276.
Tilbury. II. 281.
Timoneda, Juan. II. 183.
Tividale. I. 107. II. 220.
Tom a Lin. lxxxiv.
Tom of Bedlam songs. II. 247 et seq.
"Tom Tyler and his wife." lxxxix. II. 31.
Torbay. II. 287.
"Tournament of Tottenham, the." lxxx. I. 85 et seq.
Tower of London. I. 36. II. 251.
Trailbaston, Commission of. I. 22 et seq.
Troly loly. II. 7 et seq.
Tumblers, Female. xi.
Turnball street. II. 254.
Tuttury, the bull-running of. xi et seq.

Ulster, Earl of. I. 73.
Uppingham. II. 69.

"Valentine and Orson." xxxi.
Venice. I. 118 et seq.
Vesper bell. II. 226.
Vivaldi. I. 1.
Vortigern and Rowena. xlix.

Wager, Mr. lxxxiii.
Walker, Dr George. II. 261.
Walker, Toby. II. 259 et seq.
Wallace, Sir William. I. 28 et seq.
Wallingford. I. 12.
Walton, Izaak. II. 51.
Warenne, Earl of. xliii. I. 13.
Wassail. xlvii et seq. II. 238 et seq.
Waverley. xli.
Weelkes, Thomas. I. 11.
Welsh singing. xlii.
"Wendale." I. 45.
Westminster, Abbot of. I. 119.
"Westminster Drollery." II. 280.
"Who list to lead a souldier's life," a tune. lxxxvii.

Wickliffe, John. I. 121.
William III. II. 287 et seq.
Wimbare, Dick and Urat. lxxxix et seq.
Windsor. I. 12 et seq.
Wither, George. II. 233 et seq.
Witherington, Richard. I. 109
Women. II. 35 et seq. 242 et seq.
Woodville, Anthony, earl Rivers. II. 3.
Wrennok of Doune. I. 83 et seq.
Wyatt, Sir Thomas, senior. lxiv.

Yellow emblematic of jealousy. II. 20.

The End.

www.ingramcontent.com/pod-product-compliance
Lightning Source LLC
Chambersburg PA
CBHW030256240426
43673CB00040B/984